The Chronicles of the $700 Pony

The Chronicles of the $700 Pony

Ellen Broadhurst

Illustrations by Patty Naegeli

Half Halt Press, Inc.
Boonsboro, Maryland

The Chronicles of the $700 Pony
© 2006 Ellen Broadhurst

Published in the United States of America by
Half Halt Press, Inc.
P.O. Box 67
Boonsboro, MD 21713
www.halfhaltpress.com

Cover and interior illustrations by Patty Naegeli
Editorial services by Stacey Nedrow-Wigmore and
Patricia Patton

Printed in the United States of America

Library of Congress Cataloging-in-Publication Data

Broadhurst, Ellen, 1964-
    The chronicles of the $700 pony / Ellen Broadhurst ; illustrations
by Patty Naegeli.
        p. cm.
    ISBN 0-939481-75-8
    1. Ponies--Anecdotes. 2. Horsemanship--Anecdotes. 3. Women
horse owners--Anecdotes. 4. Broadhurst, Ellen, 1964- I. Title. II. Title:
Chronicles of the seven hundred dollar pony.
    SF301.B68 2006
    636.1'6--dc22

                                                        2006023776

For Jeff, who makes it all possible.

Table of Contents

CHAPTER 1

The $700 Pony is Acquired

14h mare. Flaxen mane and tail. 6 yo. $700.

The ad in the paper stopped me in my tracks. An entire pony for $700?

I read it again, searching for hidden meaning in its few terse words.

14h. That would be a pony.
Mare. Girl pony.
Flaxen mane and tail? Blond, girl pony.
6 yo. Reasonably young, blond, girl pony.
$700. Cheap! Hmm, I wonder if they left out a zero?

Horse pricing is a tricky business. For example, well-bred baby racehorses are sold every year at the Keeneland auction. Would you care to guess the record price someone paid for one to date? Would you believe *$9.7 million*? Yes, for one horse, and a baby horse at that. One who had done nothing but been born and grow for a year. Oh, and have a very, very famous daddy. Meanwhile, back at the ranch, you can generally pick up a used Thoroughbred off the track, the same *kind* of horse that, above, went for $9.7 million, for under $400.

Despite the above example of wildly ranging prices in the horse world, $700 would be considered well below the local going rate. Most people I know, who are in the market for a new equine, budget in the high-four, low-five figures. That generally buys you something analogous in the nonhorse world to, say, a PT Cruiser. You know, a nice, well-made horse that's just a little flashy, easy to ride and will provide years of serviceable use.

I was not in the market for a horse. Five-figure, four-figure *or* three-figure. Most emphatically *not*. While I had been riding most of my life, the day the ad happened to catch my eye, my second child had been physically present on the earth for just under five weeks and my Caesarean-section scar was still itchy. I had pretty much given up riding for the three years or so I had been on broodmare duty.

But *$700?* That was just so, well, *cheap*. I mean, if it had any redeeming qualities, it wouldn't be too hard to turn it around in a few months for a profit. A small profit, of course, because it's not like people pay five figures for a backyard pony. But a profit nonetheless. Although, in the wild-and-wooly world of horse trading, given that they were selling the thing for $700, the scenarios were endless. Potentially, it (a) was unrideable (b) had only three legs or (c) was actually an alpaca.

I glanced out the window. My horse trailer was staring back at me. I had lent it to a friend while I was otherwise occupied in the human reproductive arena. It had been returned earlier that morning all waxed and shiny, just glowing with good health.

I looked down at the ad again. If I were honest with myself, I *had*, in a small, sneaky, hadn't-really-mentioned-it-to-my-husband-yet, just-an-idea-beginning-to-bubble-to-the-surface-kind of way, been thinking about a pony—for me. Something cheap and a little green, maybe. Something I could put some miles on and sell, so that maybe I could contribute a chunk of change to that future high-four, low-five figure equine.

Not that I'm any kind of a horse trainer, to be perfectly clear. But I had successfully schooled a few ponies in my younger years.

I'm not too tall and not too wide, which are important requirements if you wish to ride ponies and not get laughed at. And I compete in the equine sports of eventing and dressage in which fully grown people are generally allowed to ride ponies.

Although, there was the small issue that I had not actually ridden a horse in, oh, say, Two Children—which translates roughly into three human years.

I looked out the window again at my trailer. It was parked in our back hay field, just down the drive from the barn. Did I mention that I happen to reside on a 130 acre farm? With a barn? And that we make hay?

I picked up the phone.

I spoke with Bob, the self-proclaimed "selling agent" for the pony. Bob was effusive, jovial and was able to confirm that the young, blond, girl pony was indeed available for anyone willing to part with $700. Bob declared that she was probably not suitable for a child. But I was able to ascertain that she was possibly broke, as he indicated he was willing to ride her for me if I came by.

I handed the two wee children to my husband, told him I was off to look at a pony, hitched up my trailer and headed off.

I was almost to Bob's barn when I was nearly deafened by the auditory assault of the "1812 Overture" at super-high-plus-maximum-volume. That would be the version *with* the cannon. While the "1812 Overture" (*with* cannon) is the most annoying cell phone ring in the short history of all cell phone rings, it is the only way I have found to keep track of the blessed thing. Dainty rings just get lost in the hustle and bustle of my daily life. The occasional nasty look from someone too close when that cannon shot rings out is well worth the ability to dial the thing in my kitchen and hear it even if I left it in the barn. Or in my case, the washing machine.

It was my husband, apparently doing a little intelligence gathering. "So, you're just going to *look* at this pony?" he asked.

"Yup," I answered. Technically, what I was doing—holding my cell phone and speaking into it while driving—is not legal state of New Jersey. Instead, you are required to us device. I do own one and at some point in my life, when things settle down a bit, I will figure out how it works. Hopefully at some point prior to the technology becoming obsolete, of course. Meanwhile, I like to keep my potentially felonious phone conversations short and to the point.

"So, why do you need the trailer?"

I could see his point. He is not exactly horse savvy. I gave him a quick primer on horse shopping. "Honey, horse shopping is a serious business! You don't just see an ad in the paper, hitch up your trailer and go buy one willy nilly! It takes *months* to find the right horse! Sometimes even *years*!"

"OK. So why do you have the trailer?"

Men. They can be so dense. "Honey, I am not *buying* this pony, I am only going to *look*!"

"OK. Should I be getting the barn ready for your new pony?" he asked. "And have you thought about fencing?"

"No, no," I insisted, "You don't *understand*! I'm not coming home with a pony! I am just going to *look*! Look, I'm almost there. I'll call you when I'm on my way home."

Bob's barn had frankly seen better days. I came up with "ramshackle," "dilapidated" and "worse for wear," all without the use of a thesaurus. There was a woman loping around the ring on a young horse, with a cigarette dangling from her lips. A little different than what I was used to, perhaps, although diversity makes the world go round, I suppose.

Bob met me at the driveway. While speaking with him on the phone, I conjured up an image of a short, stocky guy wearing a very large Stetson, possibly covering a significant hair loss. In real life, Bob was a short, stocky guy wearing a very large Stetson, definitely covering a significant hair loss.

If it was possible, he was more effusive and jovial in person than he had been on the phone, shaking my hand and bellowing, "Bob Peck at your service! Please to meet ya, young lady! Hee. Hee. Hee." Grown men really should not giggle. Particularly if they are covering significant hair loss with a rather large Stetson.

Bob led me into the barn for a first look at the $700 pony. I have to say that I was a little taken back by his sales presentation. Most people I know who sell horses try to present the animal's "best face" when meeting a potential buyer. You know, they spiff the thing up a bit, give it a bath, make sure its mane and tail are pulled and tidy, perhaps give it a quick manicure, pedicure and, if appropriate, highlights, and generally try to make sure that it is looking its best.

Bob took more of a "What-you-see-is-what-you-get" (WYSIWYG) approach. The $700 pony had certainly not been bathed—probably never in her lifetime. I wasn't sure she had even been brushed. Ever. She did at least have two shoes on. One in front and one in back.

The WYSIWYG thread ran through Bob's entire sales presentation of the pony. First, Bob pointed out a rather significant crack running through her front hoof. The one *with* the shoe, to be perfectly clear. The hoof had some kind of device that seemed designed to hold the hoof together until the crack grew out. He seemed a little discomfited that he had not mentioned this on the phone, but I had to wonder exactly how would he have described this thing to me? Frankenhoof was the best I could come up with.

He also pointed out that the pony had two huge girth sores, one on each side. I shrugged my shoulders and indicated it was not my problem, as *he* was going to ride her, not me, pointing to the general vicinity of where my Caesarean-section scar was. The good news about the girth sores, of course, was that it meant she had probably worn a saddle and had had a rider on her within the past couple of days.

Bob put what was possibly the only English saddle in the place on the pony's back and took her outside to the riding ring where the Marlboro Woman was still loping around. She had apparently stopped long enough to light up a fresh cigarette. She saw us coming, gave the pony a nasty look, downshifted and exited the ring.

The pony, in the full light of day, was as described and about what you would expect for $700. She had a rough kind of head that left her a little short of cute. She had a flat, longish back that made me wonder if there was some American Saddlebred in her otherwise-random pedigree. Overall, she certainly didn't look abused in any way, but there was something, I don't know, just a little lonely about her. She looked more *uncared* for than neglected—like a house that has been standing empty for too long.

The one thing she did have going for her, standing there in the muddy riding ring in all of her scruffy glory, was a spectacular blond tail. It was thick and long and just the right shade of flaxen to highlight her bright chestnut coat. Although when shopping for a horse that sort of thing ranks right up there with back seat cup holders—a bonus, but you no more buy a horse because it has a pretty tail than you buy a car for the sole purpose of providing your mother-in-law with a cozy place to put her coffee cup.

Bob picked up a lunge line and whip and explained that he thought it would be nice for me to see her gaits before he got on her. Now, if you are unfamiliar with this particular device, the concept is simple. A lunge line is a long rope that you clip to your horse's bridle or halter. You then stand in the middle of a 20-meter-

or-so-circle while your ostensibly well-trained equine walks, trots and canters quietly around you in response to voice, hand or whip signals. It is all very civilized and shows a superior level of training. At least that's how it works where I come from.

Bob was from a slightly different school. He attached the lunge line to the $700 pony's bridle and waved me back. I stepped back, providing sufficient room for the requisite 20-meter circle. He waved me farther back. I stepped farther back, providing more than sufficient room for the requisite 20-meter circle. He waved me back still farther, with which I decided that discretion was the better part of valor and stepped to the outside of the riding ring, closing the gate behind me.

Once I was safely out of range, Bob let go of the pony. He took the precaution of jamming his Stetson down low over his eyes and then with a flourish worthy of Siegfried and Roy, swung the lunge whip in the air, bellowing "YYYYIIIIIIPPPEEEEE" at the top of his lungs.

I have to say I was impressed. The pony went from 0 to 60 in 2.3 seconds. No wonder the Marlboro Woman left when she saw us coming. The pony rocketed by in a chestnut flash, followed by the spectacular bloom of her blond tail. The point of this exercise, I should point out, was to demonstrate what kind of a mover she was. Zipping past with her nose straight up in the air, she resembled not so much a future eventing prospect as a giraffe on crack.

Bob was clearly enjoying himself. He dug his heels in the middle of the circle, hanging onto the lunge line with one hand, swinging the whip with the other, letting off the occasional, "YYII-IPPPPPEEEEE!", when he sensed some minute reduction in speed on the part of the pony. While I was getting a pretty good view of the pony's ability to corner at high speed, this was not actually one of my buying criteria.

I waved to him, "Yoo, hoo!" He either couldn't hear me over the thunder of the pony's hooves or his own adrenaline high had gotten the better of him. I jumped up and down a few times waving my hands in the air. The apparently terrified pony spied my antics out

of the corner of her eye and seeing a new threat in my flailing self, leapt, swerved, and like some crack-addled linebacker, almost took out Bob. Not one to be intimidated by a mere 800 pounds of steam-rolling equine, Bob, flung himself around, thereby realigning the pony so that she was now galloping headlong in the *opposite* direction.

He looked over at me and yelled, "Pretty well trained, huh?"

"That's great!" I yelled back, "You can, er, *stop* now!"

Reeling her in like he was landing a tuna, Bill was able to finally slow the pony by decreasing the size of her circle to a few meters. Panting, the pony finally stood still, trembling and gazing apprehensively at Bob. He patted her fondly on the neck and turned to me, looking pretty well pleased with himself, "Fast little bugger, isn't … ARGH!" He had left his hand resting on her neck after his proprietary pat. She bit him.

Maintaining a reasonable semblance of professionalism in the face of what turned out to be the loss of a fairly good size chunk of flesh, Bob asked me to hold her while he cleaned out the wound.

At that point I was wishing I was back at home with my two wee children. My impression of the pony thus far was of some kind of psycho-speed-freak carnivore. And I hadn't seen anything yet that would make me think that she might make a good dressage or eventing pony.

She stood quietly, still panting and glaring warily now at me. I wasn't sure if it would be safer to be closer to her or farther away. I ultimately decided, weighing the whole discretion and valor thing that maybe I should try to lunge her myself, just to see what would happen.

Positioning myself carefully and watching both her teeth and her heels, I clucked to her. She walked off and marched around me in a pretty decent approximation of a 20-meter circle. So far, so good. In fact, it was much nicer than I had anticipated, although she still bore a striking resemblance to a miniature giraffe, with her neck stuck straight up in the air, which if you are looking for an event pony, on a scale of 1–10 would qualify for about a minus 4.

But in her case, the neck-straight-up-in-the-air-thing was a training issue. From a conformation standpoint, her neck was set on pretty well, indicating that with proper training, her giraffe-like profile could be rehabilitated. What I was looking for were her natural gaits. She actually had a pretty nice walk, overtracking naturally by a good two hoof prints. I eased her up to a trot. It sure wasn't Olympic material, but it's not like I was looking to go the Olympics on a $700 pony.

All in all, once you got over the significant training, or perhaps lack thereof, issues, she had a fairly nice way of going. I reeled her in and got her going in the opposite direction for a bit. She was behaving reasonably well, which is to say, she was acting almost as though she had never actually been on a lunge line before, but was trying her darndest.

And that tail, I have to say, was growing on me. It was so blond and full, and just kind of floating out there behind her. It was quite lovely. Not that I would ever choose a car because it had nice cup holders in the back seat, mind you, but it just so happens that mine does.

Bob returned with his hand well scrubbed and bandaged. He was eyeing my lunging skills critically. Clearly I did not measure up to his standards. Bob clapped his hat a little more securely on his head with his remaining good hand, "Ya want me to take her for another spin for ya?"

While it would have been a good idea to see someone actually ride her to ascertain that she was, in fact, broke at all, I was feeling a little sorry for her. Not to mention that the girth sores made me think somebody, somewhere, somehow, had at least been on her back. I stopped her. She stood quietly, looking at me fearfully. I patted her on the neck. At least she didn't bite me. Sighing, I unhooked the lunge line from her bridle and led her back into the barn, keeping a careful distance from her teeth.

Bob started in on his sales pitch: "Quick little thing, isn't she? Nice burst of speed when she starts out. And some stamina!" Bob apparently had some notion that I was planning to qualify her for the Kentucky Derby. He was missing the point that I was much more concerned that I wouldn't be able to slow her down. "Ya know, there were a couple of people here looking at her this morning. They said they'd give me a call back this afternoon, and we have more people coming later this evening."

I nodded absently at his pitch. Pretty standard. It was very possible that people had come this morning and that people were coming tonight. I sighed. She was on the crossties, still panting and glaring at Bob. I tentatively patted her neck again.

"The people this morning, now they were pretty serious about her, you know, so you might want to be thinking about making a decision on her. A nice pony like this won't hang around for long,"

I just stared at her standing there on the crossties. Actually, my thought was just the opposite—that she *would* hang around for a long time. And that since winter was nigh upon us, Bob would get tired of feeding her. From my brief experience with her, she had some pretty significant issues. She sure wasn't suitable for a kid, and there aren't many adults who ride ponies.

I walked around her again—carefully, as she swished a warning with that gorgeous blond tail. She watched me warily. She probably wasn't really nasty, despite her flesh-eating tendencies. She was just a pony who had never had a chance and quite possibly might never get one. In the wrong hands, her life would probably be quite Hobbesian—nasty, brutish and short. And since she was advertised in the local paper for $700, the odds that someone who really had no idea what he was doing could end up with her was all too real.

But, what if someone took a little time with her? Someone who really needed to get back into riding anyway. Maybe someone who had a little experience reschooling bad ponies. And maybe if she were schooled to the point where a child could ride her and learn on her, she could have a reasonably good life. Shoot. I was talking to myself. Time to fish or cut bait.

I looked at the pony. She glared back at me.

"So," I sighed turning to Bob and pulling my checkbook out of my back pocket, "who should I make the check out to?"

And the $700 Pony was mine.

CHAPTER 2

The $700 Pony Comes Home and Then Is Summarily Booted

Are you wondering if there was a missed opportunity here? Are you wondering why I didn't dicker and perhaps bring home a *$600* pony? While I do consider insisting that Bob throw in her dry-rotted bridle and super-fancy, green, nylon nonbreakaway halter a form of negotiation, I did not wrangle on the price. I mean, $700 is far enough below the going rate for ponies in my neck of the woods that I really thought she was worth it. But then, negotiation has never really been my strong suit.

The next phase of $700 Pony ownership was getting the thing in the trailer. I was mildly concerned that this might be an issue. But as it turned out, Bob, who now that he had a check in hand, really did seem to want to see her leave as quickly as possible, was prepared. Basically, he distracted me by pointing out other livestock that were available for quick sale (Hey, there were two stalls in my trailer!) while four husky guys each grabbed a corner of the Pony and heaved her up the ramp. The Pony was locked and loaded before it even occurred to her that she was entering a new phase of her life.

I drove out of the barn feeling a weird euphoria. I just bought a pony! For $700! *Wahoo!* And it felt like such a good deed!—a mercy purchase, as it were. The poor critter could get some good schooling under her girth and maybe have a whole new chance at life!

I couldn't have been more than four miles down the road when buyer's remorse set in. The feeling coincided with the Pony's beginning to kick the heck out of my trailer. And part of what I was feeling, as you might well imagine, was some angst around the need to call my husband. Luckily, he knows me pretty well.

He picked up the phone on the first ring, "So, do we own a pony?"

I was in an indefensible position. "Well, yes."

"So I really should get out to the barn and see what I can do about clearing some space for it, shouldn't I?"

I checked. Yep, my position was still indefensible. "Well, yes."

"Alrighty then. See you in a few." Good man, I have to say.

I stopped at Agway to pick up some feed and bedding. Breathing deeply while trying to figure out what in the heck a $700 pony might like to eat and sleep on, the reality of what I had done was setting in. I had willy-nilly bought myself a pony. And it was time to be a little more realistic; I really had no place to keep her.

I mentioned earlier that I live on 130 acres, and on those 130 acres there is a barn. Did I also mention that the barn is rotting and in need of major renovation? The Amish crew we hired to renovate the barn were due any day. And had been for almost 18 months.

There were some structures in the barn that the former owner of our farm had referred to as "stalls" during those heady days when we were still unburdened by 130 acres. Reviewing it mentally as my shaking hands were signing a check for my Agway order, I wondered if it was really suitable for equine habitation. Surely it would be suitable for a $700 pony? Surely there couldn't be much that was a step down for this $700 pony, could there?

And on the subject of confining the $700 Pony, did I mention that on those 130 acres there wasn't anything that you could really describe as "fencing?" Not one post, not one rail, not one strand of wire (for which I am actually pretty grateful).

Standing by the pickup, I placed another call to my husband. I was at Agway, so if there were fencing type items I should get, now would be a good time to know. "Um, hon, hey, I'll be home in a little bit. Do you have any, um, ideas on, um, fencing?" He's pretty smart, and I was guessing from our earlier conversation that he had at least been thinking about it.

"Well," he said, "what about the step-in electric mobile chicken pen?"

Aha! Brilliant! I knew I married him for a reason. It hadn't even occurred to me, but we sure did have about 300 feet of electric step-in plastic web fencing. We keep about 150 layers and sell our eggs locally. The girls are free ranging, which in our neck of the woods actually means that they live inside a portable electric fence. Portable so that we can keep moving them onto fresh pasture. Electric to keep the chickens in and the chicken-eating predators, number one being our dog, out.

While I wasn't quite sure I had ever seen anything quite like our chicken fencing around an equine before, with no other options presenting themselves, I decided a paradigm shift was in order. Of course the chicken fencing would be perfect for the $700 Pony! Shoot! Why not!? It was electric, right? So there should be no problem keeping the Pony inside it, and she would be out on fresh grass—with the chickens. What $700 pony wouldn't want to live with 150 layer hens? Ponies are social animals, right?

The Agway order was loaded into the back of the pickup and with the Pony continuing to kick the heck out of my poor trailer, I hit the road again.

With my husband diligently working on the barn, the issue of fencing ostensibly solved, and feed and bedding loaded into the back of the pickup, my brain turned to the next problem on my list: I needed to call my trainer/therapist and confess what I had done.

Now most people who ride have a trainer. It goes without saying to those who are entrenched in the horse world that if you ride, you probably do it badly and need someone on the ground on a regular basis to remind you of that fact. OK, that might be a little harsh, but just about everyone I know who rides has a trainer who ostensibly is helping them "improve," but in truth is probably just there to keep them from getting killed.

And there are some people in the horse world who are lucky enough to have a real, licensed therapist, which all horse people should be required to have because, as my husband points out, the vast majority of horse people are certifiable.

I, however, am lucky enough to have a trainer who, although she is not technically certified in the field of human psychotherapy, is one of those honest and straight-to-the-point people who just calls them as she sees them. This is invaluable in the horse world where hordes of people make a living doing something I would describe as "blowing smoke."

My trainer/therapist and I have been together for many years, and she had provided wise counsel in regard to my last horse. That horse was (and actually still is) a lovely creature, totally unsuitable for either me or my competition desires. The mare and I had managed to get along for a decade or so before my trainer/therapist was finally able to convince me that the mare really needed to find a new person who could help her fulfill her equine dreams, and I needed a horse who was frankly a little more patient and talented and could make up for my incredible lack of riding talent.

Yes, in the horse world lingo, I needed a "packer." Now for those of you looking for a little more information on this topic, a "packer" is an honest, good-natured horse who has many years of quality training under his belt and is willing to "pack around" a basically talentless amateur. A packer is safe, secure and generally fairly expensive. And while my husband and I had talked about the acquisition of a packer, the price tag of these horses was a little intimidating for both of us. I had given up my very comfortable, well-paying corporate job with the advent of farm and children and now sold eggs for a living. So the idea of buying myself a PT Cruiser equivalent frankly made me uncomfortable.

And if none of this makes any sense given that I had just bought and paid for a carnivorous, possibly barely-broke-to-ride green pony, well, welcome to my world.

Hands shaking, I dialed her number—while driving the trailer. Not a good idea. This is probably why talking on your cell phone in New Jersey is illegal.

"Guess what!" I yelled with an air of obviously false bravado, when she picked up the phone. "I bought a pony! For $700!"

"You did what?"

"I bought a pony! For $700!" I was actually pretty sure she had *heard* me the first time around, so I'm not exactly sure why I felt the need to repeat what I had said. But recognizing that whatever I said next was not going to put me on any better footing, I think I was probably stalling.

"Right. Got that."

Pause.

She wanted details. Deep breath. "Well, she's very cute! Chestnut mare, with a very nice tail. Very pretty blond!"

Silence.

More silence.

She wanted more details. "Well, she's not really very broke. I don't think. But she's very, er …" my brain flashed back to the look on Bob's face when she removed the chunk of flesh that he probably hadn't really had any desire to see go *"sweet!* Yes, she's very sweet!"

"You bought a …" she paused as though calculating what it would cost her to fire me as a client right then and there, "*Chestnut? Pony? Mare? Unbroke?*"

There is a saying the horse world that goes something like, "Chestnut mare, beware!" Basically, the rule of thumb is that mares are a little wacky (it is a hormone thing) and chestnuts are the dingyest of the bunch. Ponies, of course, are inherently evil. It's just in their DNA.

There was that indefensible position again. "Hee. Hee. Hee." Grown women really should not giggle. "Yup! For $700!"

"Let me get this straight," she sighed the deep sigh of the long suffering. "You went out and bought what would basically be considered the Axis of Evil of the horse world, and you're all excited because you only had to pay $700 for it?"

She had a point. Probably several. And I could guess there were more coming. Indefensible position or not, I was luckily about to drive into a cell-less zone, "Oh, got to go, about to lose you!" And I hung up the phone.

Seconds after leaving the cell-less zone, my ears were assaulted by the "1812 Overture." **BOOM!** Gosh, I love that cannon. It was my mom, who was just checking in.

Ah, a safe zone! My mother forgives all! *"Mom! I just bought a pony!! For $700!"*

My mother was suitably impressed. "Why, that's so nice! And will you keep it on the farm?" You've got to love mothers. When everyone else is pointing out your rather obvious failures, mothers can make you feel all warm and fuzzy.

"Yup, just pulling in the driveway now. Got to go, call you later!"

While a little of the original euphoria of the $700 Pony purchase had returned with the advent of my mother's call, my mood popped like a balloon as I drove the thumping trailer down our driveway.

Reality can be an ugly thing.

My husband was busy clearing away the junk that cluttered the "stall," with one wee child strapped to him and the other happily encrusting himself with chicken poo while hanging out with our 150 layer hen babysitters. The "stall" that my imagination had somehow transformed into something suitable for a $700 pony was smaller than my trailer and had incorporated into its structure a sufficient volume of chain link fencing for me to think that the former owner had gotten a good deal from a prison bankruptcy sale.

The exterior fencing issue that I had so blithely paradigm shifted over was unworthy of a paradigm shift. In the cold light of day there was simply no way to get the $700 Pony in and out of the step-in electric mobile chicken pen without taking the entire structure down and putting it back up each and every time. Which you simply cannot do without putting the chickens back in the barn. Have you ever tried to put 150 chickens anywhere? It makes herding cats look like child's play. Cats work primarily at ground level. Chickens can fly.

But the Pony was mine—all $700 of her. And with that reality pecking at my brain, not to mention the Pony kicking away at the inside of my trailer, we got to work on making the eminently unsuitable as suitable as possible—at least temporarily. Clearing away the junk, we were able to make a path through which to lead the Pony to her chain-link shelter, I bedded her concrete stall rather deeply in a pitiful effort to provide her some comfort, fluffed up some lovely hay from our loft, and hung her brand-spanking-new Agway feed and water buckets appropriately full of fresh feed and water.

I had naturally left in her in the trailer while we were working on her habitat. I mean, it's not like there was anywhere else to put her—besides the kitchen, of course. She had her head stuck out the side door of the trailer, ears pinned, kicking. THUMP! THUMP! I crossed my fingers that she was kicking with the hind foot that was missing a shoe. She pinned her ears back further at my approach and glared warily at me. At least she didn't try to bite. Thinking that I would rather have her wandering loose than get kicked, I unhooked the trailer tie, draped the lead rope over her neck, dropped the tailgate and butt bar, and let her figure out how to get herself out of the trailer. She approached the problem with enough studied caution that I wondered if she had ever been on a trailer before.

Once disembarked, she looked about with a less-than-thrilled expression on her face. Not that I could blame her. Squeezing past the junk in the barn, I was pretty glad she was a pony. Any taller or any wider and she would not have fit. She barely had enough room to turn around in her "stall," although it would appear she would have enough room to lie down. I wasn't too sure she could get up again, but the deal was done.

As she settled in, I debated leaving her halter on. While I would not normally leave a horse in its stall with a halter on, particularly given that this model of halter would break her neck if she got caught on anything, the latching systems for stall, barn and court-yard leading to our driveway could not be described as "robust." However the combination of chain-link fencing and her nonbreak-away nylon halter gave me a serious enough case of the shakes that I decided halterless she would be.

I crossed my fingers and locked the stall-like structure by tying the door shut to the most convenient chain link, shut the barn door from the outside, tied the "gate" from the courtyard to the driveway with some handy-dandy baling twine, and then our little family trooped back to scrape the chicken poo off our eldest child and set-tle in for dinner. Anyone notice the use of foreshadowing here? Anyone?

We had just finished getting cleaned up in the house, when my husband glanced outside. It was in those final moments before the sun gives its last yawn and stretch before calling it a night. "Honey," he said, "I think the Pony's out."

And there she was, a halterless chestnut flash galloping past the window. Darkness fell with a final resounding thud as she careened by, flicking that awesome blond tail.

With great haste, we abandoned dinner, gathered wits, a flash-light, halter, lead rope and a bucket of grain and headed out into the moonless night. My husband, a wise and patient man, but not all that well versed in the ways of equines, decided that his best move would be to hop in the car with the children and drive around our fields trying to spot her in the headlights. I had visions of him mow-ing her down but decided that it would be safer if he were in a mov-ing vehicle rather than hiking around in the dark carrying our two wee children looking for a pony who is known to find the taste of human flesh appealing.

I took the feed and headed off on foot to where I last saw her tail flickering in the final light of day. Luckily she hadn't decided to start on some ill-thought-out long journey home to Bob. She was munching grass right around where we had last seen her. A shake of the grain bucket and she was mine.

So there we stood, the $700 Pony and I, watching the glowing headlights and taillights that were my husband and two wee children eerily meandering around our 130 acres. Sometimes the headlights came closer, sometimes they were as far as half a mile away, but he never got close enough to see me, and I had no way of letting him know the Pony had been caught. Two cell phones would have solved this crisis, but while ours are equipped with state of the art Bluetooth technology, we are still impatiently waiting for the next generation of telepathic technology.

I tried jumping up and down and waving, but the flashlight was dim. I even tried a trick I have used to bring him running in the past—hopping in an unused vehicle and honking the horn. I succeeded in scaring the living daylights out of the Pony; I was not successful in bringing my husband and children in from the cold.

So we waited, and eventually he gave up. It was well before midnight, but certainly past the children's bedtime. "Next time," I scolded him, in a classic pot-calling-the-kettle-black move, "bring your cell phone!"

He looked at me as though I had sprouted a second head, "Next time?"

CHAPTER 3

The $700 Pony Goes To the Vet

She didn't get out again until the next morning. Or maybe she did get out again right away and we just found her the next morning. Whatever. She was out again when we trooped down to the kitchen for breakfast, exhausted from our late-night ramble.

I was able to catch her myself with grain bucket and lead rope, so there was no reenactment of the previous night's tragic events. But it was quickly becoming apparent that the $700 Pony would need a new home, at least temporarily, until we got the barn renovated, and maybe put in some fencing.

I gave up all pretense of worry about her hanging herself on the nylon halter. If she was going to play Houdini, she was going to have to risk a broken neck. And while she did make a few more breaks for it, I also started leaving her out with the chickens rather than having her cooped up inside her tiny stall. While it was a pain-in-the-neck hassle to get her into the chicken fencing, clearly she was used to the great outdoors. She seemed to find some comfort in being outside and in the company of 150 laying hens.

I began the week determined to achieve the critical objectives of (a) finding the $700 Pony a boarding home for the winter (preferably one with an indoor ring. Hey, if you're going to pay to board a pony for the winter, you might as well be able to ride it, right?) (b) getting the Pony to the vet and (c) moving the Pony to her new home.

Notice that (b) came before (c). Well, I suppose, technically (b) always comes before (c), doesn't it? But what I meant is that notice that "get to vet" comes before "move pony?" That would be because the Pony did not come with a Coggins. I mean, really, what do you expect for $700?

If you are shocked and appalled by that statement (by which I mean "the Pony did not come with a Coggins"), you are probably aware that it is a huge no-no to sell a horse without one. I had already written the check and haggled over the dry-rotted bridle and green nylon halter when it occurred to me to remind Bob that the law of our fine state required that he hand over the Coggins with the horse. He hemmed and hawed and said, sure, sure, she had one somewhere. But his body language suggested that the likelihood that I would get a Coggins out of him was about as likely as he was to offer me a money-back guarantee on the $700 Pony.

I must have been under the spell of adrenaline-driven euphoria when I wrote out that $700 check, because I actually drove out of the driveway with the Pony in my trailer *without* the Coggins. It is as illegal to drive around New Jersey with a horse in your trailer without a Coggins as it is to drive around yakking on your cell phone. Maybe my husband has a point about horsepeople.

I'm guessing I could have gotten away with sticking her at some boarding barn without the requisite Coggins. Most people around here would just assume you have one and don't actually ask to see it. And since it was November at this point, it wasn't like there was a huge risk of contagion if there were a one-in-a-billion issue. But if you were me, would you risk it? I mean, if your horse were the one to show up positive, wouldn't you breathe a huge sigh of relief if it were living with chickens instead of other equines?

And so (b) getting her to the vet to get her shots and a negative Coggins came before (c) moving her to a new facility (preferably with indoor). And now you might be wondering, don't most people with large animals, like horses, have the vet come to them? Of course! But I do think we can agree that in this situation, there were, well, a few extenuating circumstances?

I mean, really, if *your* pony was living in a glorified chicken coop, surrounded by hot chicken wire and chain-link fencing wearing an nonbreakable nylon halter, would you have the vet stop by? My concern was that my good vet would be on the phone to the Animal Control people before she got out of the driveway. So rather than trying to prep her for the worst, explaining over and over again that this horrific condition was just a temporary thing, I decided discretion was the better part of staying out of jail and I would drive the Pony over to the clinic myself.

In addition, it would save the barn-call fee, wouldn't it? So I called and made the appointment.

The search for a barn was, I imagine, pretty typical. I called everyone I knew and asked them to recommend a barn close to my farm. Nobody knew of any, so I went to the Yellow Pages. I called every farm that looked like it might board horses. I left messages on half a dozen answering machines, and no one ever called me back.

I went to three local tack stores and pulled those tiny phone number tags off every "boarding" sign that looked like it might be within a reasonable distance (and if you have ever done this, you know that three out of four don't include an actual location). And no one ever called me back.

I even *drove* to a couple of the properties, bringing with me my very own white board marker, and left notes on their white boards, *begging* someone to call me back. And no one ever called me back.

And so, several days into the hunt, I had an appointment for the vet scheduled, but still no place to put the Pony.

The poor $700 Pony might still be living with her new 150 best chicken friends if not for my township's Municipal Agricultural Advisory Committee. Now, your town might not be lucky enough to have its very own agricultural committee, but mine does, and I am a groupie. They meet once a month at the town hall and their mission is to provide a voice for agriculture in our community. I go every month and represent the public. Usually I am the only public present, so they even let me sit at the table with them.

And when we get to the "public input" part on the agenda, they always turn to me and ask if I have anything to say. I usually don't, but this particular evening, I figured, if anyone can help me, this group could, and I related my inability to locate a barn for the $700 Pony. One of the committee members said she had a nice barn *with* an indoor, mentioned a monthly boarding fee that would not make my checkbook weep silently every month and the deal was done.

I did make a quick barn call the next day, just to make sure that her idea of "nice barn" and mine were in alignment. I have to admit, I was quite pleasantly surprised when I drove up the driveway. I personally would not have described the barn as "nice." Maybe super nice? Maybe nicer than nice? Maybe it even qualified as fancy-schmancy nice? It was certainly the nicest barn I had ever boarded at, and since the Pony would be back to our renovated barn next, probably the nicest barn I would ever be in.

All that stood between the $700 Pony and an indoor ring was a simple trip to the vet.

And now I will let you in on a little secret about me: I am an efficiency machine.

The $700 Pony needs to go to the vet. The dog *also* needs to go to the vet. The only time my vet can see both is on the day and time usually set aside for my son's playgroup. So I scheduled my ever-patient mom to come down to watch both children and scheduled playgroup to be *at my house* while I take said Pony and dog to the vet at the same time. Brilliant!

And now, with the help of that happy bastard, Hindsight, let's revisit the above thinking: the $700 Pony needs to go to the vet so she can have shots and draw blood for Coggins so she can move to the fancy-schmancy facility (*with indoor*) that has agreed to take her scruffy green self for a sum equal per month to more than my layer hens and I bring in during a year (yeah, employed husband!).

Pony will *probably* load on trailer because she loaded on trailer when I bought her. I have conveniently blocked out that it actually took four husky men to hustle her onto the trailer, but despite my startling efficiently, I have been known to overlook a detail now and again. I had planned to load her a few times preemptively, but the best-laid plans of mice and men are often foreshortened by warfarin. Or something like that.

The dog needs to go to the vet immediately for her annual rabies shot in order to meet our annual dog registration date. We live in a town that would make John Mellencamp feel like a big-city boy. If you register a dog in 2005 and fail to register it in 2006, at some point when our local officers of the law are not too busy (i.e., Monday through Sunday), they will stop by to see if said dog has expired or if you are in violation of the local dog registration ordinance. The officers are great guys, and despite my illicit cell phone habits, I make a fairly concerted effort to stay on their side of the law.

The dog was an unfortunate psycho mutt who has reached the unhappy age of 7 without gaining any of the emotional maturity one expects of a dog of 7. She was begging for a lobotomy and heaven help me should I ever get in range with a nail gun.

My son and his playgroup were a delightful, frolicking group of 2-year-olds. They are such a *hoot!* For those of you not well acquainted with human offspring, think "weanlings." Joyful, gamboling, boisterous and nearly impossible to contain.

I am a moron.

First, for animal-welfare-concern reasons outlined above, I was hauling the $700 Pony to the vet. My trailer is a gooseneck. This meant that Psycho Mutt was going to be riding *inside the truck* with me. *Merde!*[1]

Stoically, I loaded Psycho Mutt in the cab. Unfortunately, Psycho Mutt and I do not have the best relationship, in part, because while she and I share a fondness for chickens, I am their caretaker and nurturer, while she runs them down and slaughters them in cold blood. Can you see the problem?

---

[1] This word is French. I would like to think that the occasional use of French in this narrative would reveal my elevated level of sophistication. Unfortunately, this particular French word means "poo."

Dogs and their relationships to people, I would like to point out, exist on an interesting continuum. They range basically from "Dog as Surrogate Child" to "Dog as Farm Implement." Can you guess on which end of the spectrum Psycho Mutt resides? I'll give you a hint: if my haybine suddenly went berserk and started killing chickens, I'd be in the market for a new haybine. Ah, well, Psycho Mutt and my husband were a package deal. Enough said on that topic.

I was not excited about having her ride in the cab with me. And unfortunately, she was so excited about going for a ride in the truck (despite the fact that the *only* place she ever goes is to the vet—more than one can short of a six pack, this one) that I was a little concerned that the adrenaline rush was going to blow her puny brain right out through her ears. Instead, she limited herself to flinging herself around the pickup cab with supreme abandon, spraying canine saliva all over the inside of my truck. Ew.

Second, I have not actually had time to see if the $700 Pony will, in fact, get back on the trailer. Of course, the $700 Pony does not want to get in the trailer. Why would she? She has no desire to leave her 150 new best chicken friends behind, right?

Third, the trailer was within sight of the cavorting 2-year-old playgroup. Small human children are the most adorable little things—at least, if you are their parents. Probably less so if you are a $700 pony.

So there I was with grain and lunge whip in hand slowly coaxing the $700 Pony onto the ramp when the pack of little darlings caught sight of the $700 Pony.

All heck broke loose.

Mommyponyponyponyponypony!" "*Horsiehorsiehorsiehorsie!*" "*Neighneighneighneigh!*" and then, of course, my son who has the inside track: "*That'smymommy'sponymommy'sponymommy'spony!*"

They looked like a pack of young Thoroughbreds at the track, barely restrained by their outriders, until, unlike at the track, they broke free from their mommy handlers and in a swarming mass, charged down the hill toward me and the unfortunate $700 Pony.

Psycho Mutt, seeing the seething mass of 2 year olds, lost her mind completely and, I *swear*, tried to turn herself *inside out*! And *nearly succeeded*! All you could see in the cab of the truck was a frenzy of flying fur and saliva as she flung herself against the door again and again, hoping against hope that a miracle would occur—that she would discover she had grown an opposable thumb and would be able to let herself out of the cab.

I looked at the $700 Pony and she looked at me. "Pony," I said, "Now would be a really good time to just hop right on the trailer." She pondered this for a split second, glanced up at the converging mass of tiny humans, glanced at the nearly inside out canine inside the cab of the truck and hopped up into the trailer. With bare nanoseconds to spare, I hauled up the ramp, as what seemed like several hundred pounds of frenetic human two year olds, driven down the hill by the perpetual energy supplied by an overabundance of animal crackers and apple juice, *whumped* into the side of the trailer.

So, while I am a moron, the $700 Pony is not.

CHAPTER 4

The $700 Pony Is Diagnosed with Social Anxiety Disorder

Sadly, the $700 Pony suffers from social anxiety disorder.

You've seen the TV ads, haven't you? (Softly Soothing Gender Neutral Voice Over) "If you find yourself with excessive, persistent fears about upcoming social situations and if the anxiety you feel in social situations is so severe it disrupts your daily life, it is possible you are suffering from social anxiety disorder."

I immediately went to paxil.com and gave the $700 Pony the Paxil SPIN (Social Phobia Inventory) Test: are you afraid of people in authority? Yes! Do parties and social events scare you? Yes! Do you sweat excessively in front of other people? Yes! Are you afraid of doing things when people might be watching? Yes!

There you have it, classic social anxiety. Odd thing to find in a herd animal but, hey, these things happen.

Now, social anxiety might not be the number one criteria on your list if you were seeking a new eventing prospect but (verbal shrug of shoulders) what do you expect for $700? Next question: Now that we have ascertained that the $700 Pony suffers from social anxiety, what can be done about it? Well, I can tell you what *not* to do.

First, don't exacerbate the situation by having the $700 Pony live with chickens. This did nothing for her self esteem.

Second, don't make the situation worse by *then* moving the rather scruffy $700 Pony, sadly spotted with chicken poo, to the fancy-

schmancy facility (FSF) where she will be surrounded by the groomed-and-clipped-within-an-inch-of-their-little-equine-lives horse elite, not to mention a pack of rogue Jack Russell Terriers and a troop of unfailingly menacing Corgis. This will not result in an immediate decrease in social anxiety, let me tell you.

Who knew that there are *entire breeds* of canines on this planet in worse mental condition than Psycho Mutt? These two hooligan gangs rival the Bloods and the Crips for sheer testosterone run amuck, although on a significantly lower-to-the-ground scale. My perspective on Psycho Mutt is shifting in her favor. At least she is tall enough to see coming.

But I digress.

The FSF is all you may imagine. I have boarded at some nice barns in my day. Some with indoors even. Some that I would describe as "fancy." But this, *this* was fancy-*schmancy*.

There are 100—let me repeat that—*one hundred*—stalls on the property, each larger than my first condo. The horses are like none I have seen in my sheltered lifetime (although to keep it in perspective, I think a $700 pony is a *big deal*). These horses and ponies are tick fat, sleek, clipped within an inch of their lives, with gorgeous bug-eyed, sculpted heads, like horses conceived by Michelangelo, like creatures from another equine planet. Some of you may be saying, "Hey, rube lady, where have you been all your life!" Well, I have not been around anything like this.

The FSF is cared for by a super efficient team of gentlemen for whom English will someday be a second language. These guys are serious workers and keep the FSF and its resident super equines in tip-top shape. For someone used to self care, this is all a little intimidating.

The (many) grooming stalls have individual lights, fans and wet bars and are covered with this soft, rubberized brick stuff that feels a bit like a down featherbed for the feet. I thought it a little odd that there were no drains. How in the heck did these people keep super equines as spotless as they obviously were without access to water? Then I opened the door to what I thought was the bathroom.

Forgive me, I almost burst into tears. First of all, the "wash stall" was exponentially, nay, light years nicer than the single bathroom my family of four shares (although, technically, only two of us are potty trained). Hot and cold running water, insulated and yet well ventilated with an electric fan, cedar lined, unbelievably gorgeous and totally functional. Oh, and wait, there are *two* of them! Waaahh!!

But I dither. Let us swing back to our socially anxious $700 Pony, shall we?

Our trip to the vet was successful. The Pony was indeed a pony (14 hands), deemed to be about 6 years old and in fairly robust good health. Her Coggins test was indeed negative and she was duly and appropriately dewormed so as to make her a suitable healthy companion for her new group of friends at the FSF.

All settled in, I took to heading out early in the morning to work with her—very early in the morning so that my husband could stay with the children while I went out to begin teaching her everything she needed to know about being a horse. Life seemed good.

And then my trainer/therapist called.

Trainer/therapist: "So when the heck am I going to get to see you ride this mythical pony?" Trainer/therapist is located about a 45 minute trailer ride from the Pony, so I needed to schedule a lesson with her at a time when my children would be well cared for.

Me: "Well, she's going really well, despite her social anxiety issues. She's a little intimidated by her surroundings, you know, so we've been taking it easy. Lots of lunging. She has a GREAT walk! Her trot's a little quick, but that's just because she's a little, well, you, know, socially anxious. And her tail? I have mentioned her tail before, haven't I? It's really quite lovely. But overall it's going GREAT! I'm sure we'll be ready to event in the spring!"

Trainer/therapist: "So what's she like when you ride her?"

Pause the length of, oh, say, the Triassic Period (35 million years, give or take).

Me: "Ride her?"

Trainer/therapist: "You have been riding her, haven't you?"

Pause the length of, oh, say, the Jurassic Period (68 million years, give or take).

Trainer/therapist: "You have had this Pony for a month! Are you telling me you haven't ridden her yet????!!"

Pause the length of, oh, say, the Cretaceous Period (80 million years, give or take).

Me: "Um, well."

Way-too-astute-for-her-own-good trainer/therapist: "Let me ask you another trick question: I heard nice walk, OK trot. Nothing about that mysterious third gait. Do we know if it *canters*??"

Me nailed to the proverbial wall: "Um. Probably? I mean, they all do, don't they?"

Tough-love trainer/therapist: "OK, girlfriend, reality check time. You have some crazy-ass notion that you are going to *event* this pony next year: it might help if you actually threw a leg up over it and *rode it*!"

Me: "Well, I've been working on hcr social anxicty issues."

Pause the length of, oh, say, the entire Mesozoic Era (encompassing the Triassic, Jurassic and Cretaceous Periods). And longer, actually. She hung up on me.

CHAPTER 5

The $700 Pony Goes Christmas Shopping

A good friend of mine recently mentioned in a very offhand way that she thought I was a little on the anal side. I was aghasted.[2] I would be the opposite of anal. Anal people have their lives in *order*! Anal people are not up until 4 am trying to get a 14-year-old printer to print out addresses on their Christmas cards. An anal person would have realized that it would have taken less time to teach the cat to write and then have her address the cards.

No, no, I'm not anal. But I kind of wish I were, just a little.

Anal people can get places *on time,* not to mention *clean* and *tidy*—or at least some relative equine version of clean and tidy. I am one of those people who always look disheveled and like she is running late. Usually because I am.

I did decide, though, that with the advent of the $700 Pony, it was time for a fresh start. You know, one of those, today-is-the-first-day-of-the-rest-of-your-life kind of deals. I could present myself a little better at the barn, tidy up a bit, plan better to ensure I'm on time. Blah, blah. So I bought myself one of those charming little Ariat vests. Hey, you've got to start somewhere, and "A" for Ariat seemed like a fine place.

---

[2] Aghasted—while you might not recognize this word, contextually the definition is obvious. The term has a place in the hearts and minds of a certain segment of the online equine population and deserves an eventual place in the Oxford English Dictionary. And thus, its inclusion here.

Having purchased said charming Ariat vest, it was time to bite the proverbial billet and scheduled a lesson with my trainer/therapist. People were beginning to ask me if the $700 Pony was some weird delusion that I had made up in order to get invited to the barn Christmas party.

I scheduled a lesson for a week away at 10 am, and, with my resolution of being the new, improved, pulled-together me, I put together a plan for the new, improved, pulled-together $700 Pony. I mean, I really like the $700 Pony, but the truth is she looks a lot like a $700 pony. She needed at least two parts elbow grease and one part Cowboy Magic™ to get her looking more like a, say, $750 pony. So the plan was follows: (a) trace clip her, (b) pull her mane, (c) wash her tail and (d) clean my tack.

It goes without saying that none of this happened. I have two tiny children. For those of you who do not have experience with human children, imagine that you have four female dogs who have all whelped at the same time, each bearing 12 puppies. The bitches have rejected the puppies and you have to hand feed each of the 48 puppies, and you recently lost both of your hands in a combine accident and can't afford prosthetics. This is a close approximation of life with two tiny children.

I gave up on the trace clip when it took me four weeks to get a blanket that fit. I *finally* acquired one the day before my lesson. But, since the socially anxious $700 Pony practically faints every time I approach her with something as simple as a currycomb, I decided discretion was the better part of surviving long enough to collect Social Security and chose not to introduce her to the clipper.

She also fainted every time I tried to pull her mane. She came with a glorious long blond mane that matched her tail. Unfortunately, that sort of thing is just not *de rigueur* in my part of the horse world. We like to torture our equines by pulling their mane hair out so the mane is short and tidy. Yes, we pull it out by the roots. Seriously! In some ways it is shocking that the Pony objected to having her mane pulled out by the roots—I mean millions of horsepeople in the world do this every day! And yet on another level, who can blame her?

So I pulled a few wee hairs out every day. I figured a couple of hairs here and a couple of hairs there every day and before you knew it, she would have a tidy pulled mane. And probably by Easter, she will. OK, so her mane looked a little shaggy, not the end of the world.

As for washing her tail, well, given her reaction to basic grooming, I decided that fighting the great water battle in the dead of winter might not be such a great idea. A little Cowboy Magic™ and a brush, a quick bang and her tail looked just fine. It was really so blessed gorgeous all on its own, it was probably better I not get my knickers in a twist about it.

So now we were down to the things that can be accomplished the night before: clean the Pony and clean tack. Feeling that hefty burden that all mothers shoulder (that would be "guilt," people), I decided that my 48 orphan-puppy equivalents needed more attention than the $700 Pony, so I skipped the barn the night before and added an extra hour on the morning side for pony prep.

Are you ready for some higher math?

Lesson is at 10 am. Subtract one hour for cleaning the Pony and tack, one hour trailering and one "bonus" half hour because I am a moron and cannot possibly stick to a time schedule. I decided that I needed to leave the house at 8:30. That would be am, not pm. Anybody out there scratching their heads?

Yeah, so here's what happens: 8:30 am comes and goes as I am patting my babies on their heads, trying to locate a missing file for my husband and shouting out last-minute instructions to my mother in the proper care and feeding of tiny children. She raised me so clearly she has no idea what she is doing.

I finally hop in the truck around, say five minutes to 9, thinking, "Good thing for that bonus half hour!" I go into abrupt cardiac infarction when I see that the clock in the truck reads *five minutes to 10*!! What the?? I resume normal pulse and respiration when I realize that I never bothered to change the clock in the truck for daylight-saving time. And then return to my previous state of cardiac infarction when I realize that I have screwed up big time.

There will be no clean tack, no clean $700 Pony and it is possible there will be no lesson.

With one eye pasted to the rearview mirror, I screamed to the barn. As I have mentioned, I live in a fairly small town and I do like to keep ~~stay~~ on the right side of the law. One of the afore mentioned officers of the law and I had a business meeting a couple of years ago. His business, alas, which would be dealing with miscreants.

Specifically, it was 6 am and I was five minutes into my hour-and-15-minute commute to work, and I had had minimal sleep the prior night since my first wee child was not at that point where he slept through the night. The officer gently pointed out to me that he had clocked me doing 61 in a 40 mph zone.

I, the picture of blithe truthfulness replied, "Well, good thing you caught me when you did! I was only in fourth gear and about to shift up when I saw your lights!" After that episode, my husband and I decided it might be safer if I stayed at home with the children and took up chicken farming.

Arriving at the barn and thanking the higher powers that the FSF people had read my note and left the $700 Pony inside, I broke all land-speed records for hitching up the trailer and fled down the aisle toward the $700 Pony.

Luckily, the $700 Pony took pity on me and got right on the trailer. The list of stuff I need to take with me for a lesson is actually tattooed on my palm. (So I forgot a girth *once*, or twice, um, and a bridle, well, maybe three times now. Oh and there was that one time I left my saddle back at the barn. Well, it's not like I drown kittens, for crying out loud!). I did head out the driveway with hat, bat, gloves, saddle, girth and bridle as well as the Pony.

So there I was now flying down the road, and I reached for my cell phone to let the trainer/therapist know I was on my way, which, if you have been paying attention you know would not be on the right side of the law in the fine state of New Jersey, and luckily for me (*whew!*), my cell phone was on low battery. Ah, well, probably not a good day to stop at the Verizon store to get that car charger I have been talking about buying for the past decade. I could probably coerce them to get my handless thing working there, too, but who the heck has time for that kind of stuff? Clearly, not me.

So what's the damage? Well the one hour I had blocked out for trailering was really too much. It is less than half an hour driving in my car, so figure 40 minutes, tops, with the trailer. And it was only 9:33 and it was only half an hour lesson and my trainer/therapist didn't have another lesson until 11. So it was going to be fine. I was going to be a little late, and the $700 Pony is going to look like a $700 pony and I am going to look exactly like I usually do, except with a charming little Ariat vest on, so what the heck. All was well.

But pride cometh before a fall, does it not? Because as I was trucking along, I realized I was making better time than I had expected. So much better, in fact, that I was beginning to believe that I would pull into the driveway *really close* to 10 am. So it would be like I was not late at all, mostly. And maybe with the charming vest on, I could pull it off!

But if you have been paying attention, you can probably guess that was not what happened. And you are not going to believe what really did happen next, because I can barely believe it myself. But believe it. It really, truly happened this way.

To clarify, I have lived in this general vicinity for *years*. I have driven these roads for the past decade and a half. But let us not forget that I cannot add one hour plus one hour plus one-half hour properly.

So there I was at the stop light, ready to make the turn onto the Route 78 Interstate, counting the seconds as they ticked off on my truck clock, thinking, "Maybe, maybe, I will not be *too* late…" when I accidentally turned into the Wal-Mart parking lot.

Well, shoot! you say. How in the heck could anyone mistake a *Wal-Mart parking lot for a major New Jersey State thoroughfare??????*

Well, no matter how it happened, it happened. And there I was in the Wal-Mart parking lot with my rig. And here's the kicker, folks. It was *the week before Christmas!!* Bad time to get caught in the Wal-Mart parking lot. It was a bit like an Escher sketch. You could get in, *but there was no way out!*

I drove left—there was a monster Hummer blocking my way. I maneuvered right—there was a flock of minivans disgorging their tiny human cargo. I feinted, I jabbed, I punched, all to no avail. I was stuck in the Wal-Mart parking lot.

Desperate, I finally gave up on the seemingly simple task of turning my rig around in the Wal-Mart parking lot and made the fateful (oh, heck, why don't we just call a spade a spade: "stupid" would be a better word) decision to duck out down a small side road with the ominous sign "Dead End." Why would anyone do this, you ask? Because in my rose-colored-glasses world, I am thinking dead end = cul-de-sac = nice turn-around area.

OK, raise your hands, anyone who actually passed geometry in high school. Remember all those bloody logic theorems? Well here is a new one for you: while all cul-de-sacs are dead ends, *not all dead ends are cul-de-sacs!*

As I hauled the $700 Pony down the lonely, ever-narrowing dead-end road, I stopped every hundred yards or so to try to turn around. I tried a 43-point turn here, moved on to the next relatively wide swath of narrow dead-end roadway to try a 37-point turn. Anyone watching would have thought the rig was being driven by an idiot. They would not have been far from the truth.

Of course, it all worked out in the end. Despite my moronic miscalculation of the Wal-Mart parking lot as a major New Jersey thoroughfare and an equally village-idiot move to leaving the wide-open spaces of the parking lot for a dead-end road I was eventually able to, by sheer force of will, turn the rig around and get going in the right direction.

I did get to the trainer/therapist barn in time to squeeze in a half hour lesson. And because she knows me so well, she didn't even *ask* why I was late. Which is good, because telling her I had gotten "lost" would have been more humiliating than actually being lost. She did, however, mention that she thought my new vest was just spiffy.

CHAPTER 6

The $700 Pony is Introduced to the Golden Pathway

Did the last chapter leave you dangling? Since you have managed to hang in this far, do you have some unanswered questions? Like, for example, "*Hey*! Did you ever actually ride that pony?" Or, "So, did your trainer/therapist kick you out of her barn like she *should* have for doing something as utterly moronic as buying a green pony that you are clearly not able to ride? And since she probably didn't, what did she think of the thing when she finally saw it?"

When we finally arrived at the trainer/therapist's barn for our lesson via the Wal-Mart parking lot, it was, in fact the first time the trainer/therapist laid eyes on the Pony. And it was darn near one of the first times I actually got on her back and rode her.

It has been pointed out to me that my grasp of reality is tenuous at best—pointed out by people who actually like me and are generally in pretty close contact with my life, that is, like my mom, my husband, and the trainer/therapist. "Delusional" is another word that gets tossed around a lot. They mean it in a *nice* way, of course, I think, although I do wish they would use more positive words like "hopeful" or "overly optimistic."

Well, I *am* hopeful. It was with great *hope* that I purchased the Pony (Did I mention that I only paid $700 for this pony?), despite the fact that I had promised my trainer/therapist that I would never, ever, ever, torment a green horse again. And despite the fact that I had not actually ridden a horse in, oh, say, Two Children (translating roughly into 3 Human Years).

While I had been making a great show of heading off to the barn every morning and letting my fine husband rise with our two wee children, I wasn't logging much actual time in the saddle. Truth be told, the thing had not demonstrated much that would lead me to believe she had much time with anyone on her back. And since the closest thing to a saddle that I had been near for the past three years were the stirrups in the Ob-Gyn's office, well, I was actually afraid that I might do more harm than good.

Don't get me wrong; I had been on her back a few times. The resume that Bob presented when I bought her was that she had spent her working years as a trail pony for a family in one of the northernmost states in the Union. Apparently the family had a large farm but had not been all that horsy. So the Pony had been trail ridden on alternate Sundays in months not containing the letter "R." Unfortunately, while low mileage is a bonus when you are buying a used car, *higher* mileage is generally more desirable in the horse world.

Most of the time the Pony and I spent together was on the lunge line. And most days the Pony continued to channel the ghost of Bob as her guide for appropriate lunge-line behavior. I do own a lovely lunging surcingle and so demonstrate a semi-professional look as I head out for our lunging exercise. But the Pony, who just had no positive lunging experiences to fall back on, was depending on me, a frank amateur despite my sophisticated equipment, to help her understand proper lunging behavior. My experience in starting young horses on the lunge line had always involved more than one human, so I was really struggling on the whole retraining thing.

And I *had* hopped on her after a few of our futile lunging experiences. I was in an indoor, so I figured the worst she could do was run into a wall. I had walked her around and around and even ventured a few short trots. But, man-oh-man, she was just so, well, *green*. Her steering was barely functional, she clearly never had brakes installed and she basically had two speeds: fast and faster. This was not a good combination.

And to top it all off, "brave" would not be a word I would use to describe her. For example, she was afraid of all of the jumps in the indoor. The FSF is a hunter farm, so the jumps are colorful and numerous, but they never move. Every single day she would startle (well, tried to turn and run might be more accurate) at each and every one of them. Additionally, shadows on the ground frightened her into a state of paralysis. And she tripped over every single pole she ever tried to walk over. This does not bode well, as the sport of eventing, for which she has been earmarked, does involve leaping over obstacles. And falling on your face over them does not qualify as success.

She also does this other thing—an equine Gordian Knot presented for me to solve. It's a little hard to explain, but I'll give it a go: The $700 Pony does something that from a physiological and aerodynamic standpoint doesn't seem possible, and since I have never actually seen this movement, only felt it, it's hard for me to determine how much is happening in my head and how much is reality.

Imagine a herd of gazelle on the Serengeti grazing quietly and peacefully, although ever on the alert, knowing that any lapse in attention will result in an end to grazing time—forever. Suddenly one of the delicate, sinewy creatures senses the approach of a gazelle-eating predator! The gazelle *leap* into the air, tiny little hooves all coming together to form a sort of point as their little backs round high in the air, and then somehow they propel themselves forward with a startling velocity! It's about like that.

Now this is not the first time I have been presented with an athletic mare that uses her athleticism for evil. I used to have a horse who, when she was really ticked off, would capriole. Now for those of you who have never experienced this, well, I wish I were you.

The capriole is one of the high-school movements of the Spanish Riding School. When done by professionals, the horse slowly rears up on his hind legs, pauses for just a moment and then launches himself in the air. Then, as if that were not enough, while airborne, he kicks out with his hind legs. No, I am not kidding! This is real, and there are people who *teach horses how to do this!*

My mare did it for kicks, mostly when she wanted to communicate that she was really pissed off, and I have to say that it was very effective.

The $700 Pony, however, seems to execute the "Serengeti Slide" when she is afraid of things on the ground. Things on the ground that frighten her include, but are not limited to, cavalletti, rocks, grass, leaves and the odd pile of manure (even one or two that she has deposited, truth be told). It is tough to predict when it will happen, particularly since she will race around in some pitiful geometric shape that barely resembles a circle for several laps and then, suddenly, out of the corner of her eye, note an uneven patch of footing and decide that a Serengeti Slide is in order. She has not managed to dislodge me yet, but I have been left, more often than I cared to think, clinging to her back like a tick,

But unlike Alexander, who in his pre-Great youth solved the Gordian Knot with a sword, training horses requires patience and fortitude and the ability to serenely unravel training tangles.

Generally, whacking your horse over the head with a rapier, while momentarily satisfying, is just going to piss them off.

So these were the problems thus far evident with $700 Pony. I had come for this lesson in the hopes that the trainer/therapist could offer some advice in solving them.

And thusly, when I arrived—late—to my lesson, I just put the thing on a lunge line and let 'er rip, thinking that I might as well just lay all of my cards on the table. There really is no point in trying to bluff with the trainer/therapist. If you are holding a pair of twos, hey, you might a well just fess up that you are holding a losing hand and move on.

My trainer/therapist stood watching while the $700 Pony flung herself around us in a circle at warp speed. She started whistling "The Flight of the Bumblebee."

"Come on!" I said, "Not fair! The Pony's really trying."

She glanced over at me, unimpressed.

If the trainer/therapist had a motto, it would be "Do or do not. There is no try." If that sounds familiar, you might well be a *Star Wars* fan. Yeah, Yoda, that little green critter with the big pointy ears who always sounded a little too much like Grover on *Sesame Street* for me to take seriously said it. But my trainer/therapist is a little too cut and dry to walk around spouting mottos. So I like to spout this one for her.

I reeled the Pony into the middle of the circle. The trainer/therapist sighed a deep sigh, "OK, why don't you hop up on her and we'll see what we've got."

It wasn't pretty. The Pony demonstrated her absolute lack of any training, and I did little more than hang on. "You know," she finally said, "I have never seen a horse move quite like that. She reminds me an awful lot of Pepe LePew." She paused and shook her head. "Or, no, maybe what Pepe would go like if he were a crackhead."

The trainer/therapist watched a while longer and just kept shaking her head sadly. "What, what, *what*," she finally asked exasperated as I almost fell off for the third time as the Pony executed yet another Serengeti Slide at some shadow on the ground, "were you thinking when you bought this pony?"

I was feeling a little lost and desperate myself. "Well," trying to keep the whining and sniffling out of my voice, "It's not like I haven't *done* this before! I've taken a couple of very green ponies from nothing to eventing at *Training* level, in just a few months! I'm not sure why I'm having such a hard time with this one."

"Well," she said, "let's reflect on this a moment, shall we? Look back in time a bit, as it were. Now *when* exactly did you do all of this before?"

Me, reflecting truthfully: "Well, it was a few years ago, wasn't it?"

Therapist/trainer: "You were 25."

Me, a little puzzled: "Yeah, so what's your point?"

Patient beyond words therapist/trainer: "And how old are you now?"

It hit me like a ton of feathers. Which, frankly, will knock you on your butt just as quick as a ton of bricks, because, let's face it; a ton is a ton, whether we're talking bricks or feathers.

Me: "*Holy horse poop*! I'm … I'm … I'm *40!!!!!!!* Oh, my *gosh!!!* That was, like, *FIVE CHILDREN ago*! Where has the time *gone!!????* I'm a *40 year-old mother of two riding a $700 pony??* And I think I'm going to *compete*? I'm going to look like an *idiot*!

The trainer/therapist nodded in affirmation to this last bit. Yes, indeed, there was little doubt that I was going to stand out a bit if we did actually get the $700 Pony to a couple of events. The comments I used to get at the end of a dressage test when I was in my 20s about it "*being time for my mom to buy me a full-sized horse*"[3] are just not going to happen—I don't look like I'm 12 anymore. Two tiny children will do that to you. Now I just look like a big honking 135-

---

[3] Yes, a judge really said this to me. I was 27 years old and competing a 13.2 appy pony. If someone were to say it to me today, I would probably fall on my knees in gratitude. At the age of 27, I was still being carded every time I tried to purchase alcohol, so it was less of a big deal.

pound grownup (that would have been 125 pounds Two Children ago) pounding a sweet, little pony.

But, and the trainer/therapist took a moment to bring me back to reality: I had bought and paid for the $700 Pony. And while the trainer/therapist and I did agree that I should not ride green horses anymore, this particular critter, despite the fact that she is (a) a striking shade of emerald, (b) a chestnut mare and (c) a pony, seems to have a huge streak of forgiveness embedded in her chip. She is seemingly, deep down a forgiving soul, despite my initial concern that she was a carnivore, and she does not seem to be taking my colossal ineptitude personally.

And thusly the trainer/therapist set about to introducing me and the $700 Pony to the Golden Pathway. Now the title of this chapter is "The Golden Pathway," and if you actually read and retained that bit of information from several pages ago, you might be wondering when in the heck I was planning to get around to explaining exactly what that means. Well, now.

As I have already explained, the trainer/therapist is a down-to-earth, well-grounded tough-love kind of individual. She is not the type to march about spouting mottoes and axioms and all that jazz. So, the Golden Pathway springs from my brain, which actually makes it rather suspect, given all that you know about me, does it not?

But the concept is simple, and a good one to reflect upon. Those of us in the horse world who have regular trainers generally take lessons for the simple reason that we want to progress. And progress is probably not something that we are capable of achieving on our own. So we have "regular" lessons. For some, that might mean once or twice a week, for some once or twice a month. But the point is that you spend some concentrated amount of time with your trainer and then you go off on your own and practice what he or she has tried to teach you.

Unlike many skills, which are fairly static, the skill of riding is fluid. I mean, in the sport of riding, you are basically expected to perform with something that has the brain the size of a large walnut and that outweighs you—by a lot. Can you name any other sport like that? I mean, imagine if when you played tennis the racquet took to arguing with you, or decided if and when it wanted to play? Or imagine if NASCAR race cars tried to bite each other when they got too close? Or if golf clubs turned up lame if the footing on the course wasn't just to their liking?

Well, you get my drift. When you ride, you are dealing not only with your physical and mental abilities and limitations, but you have to factor in the horse you are riding—daily. Because in riding, every horse is different, and even each different day that you ride the same horse, the horse can be different. A horse that was quiet and happy one day in the indoor ring, the very next day, if the wind is blowing, if the stars are not aligned properly or if the horse happens to have gotten a disturbing flake of hay for breakfast, can be an orangutan.

And part of the reason we riders pay homage (as well as large volumes of cash) to our trainers and trainer/therapists is that they have insights into the fluidity of equines and can give us the tools to deal with these ceaselessly changing, shifting creatures.

You want proof? If you are a rider reading this I ask, have you ever had a lesson where the following scenario occurs:

Horse does (a).

You do (b).

Trainer yells, "What the name of Sam Hill did you do (b) for?"

You reply that at your lesson last month, horse did (a) and trainer told you to do (b).

Trainer yells "That was a month ago, you moron! Jiminy Cricket, now you should do (c)!

In the name of progress, your relationship with your equine is ever shifting, ever moving, ever changing, and how you act and react changes and moves depending on the place, the horse, and the horse's mood. Maybe a good analogy is that horses are a bit like Jell-O, shimmering in the light, changing shape and form based on temperature, barometric pressure and the addition of sugar. Hmmm, come to think of it, horses are exactly like Jell-O.

Sure, there are some hard-and-fast rules, some things that are consistent from horse to horse and from day to day. Just ask any serious dressage person.[4] But the point is, if you are taking lessons and your goal is to grow and learn and refine, then you are always learning new things and, hopefully, teaching your horse new things and refining the old. So things *change*.

But back to the Golden Pathway. So at the end of a lesson where you have just spent a miserable hour cowering in the focused light of your trainer's wrath, many things have probably transpired. Possibly you have been yelled at, scolded, sworn at, picked up out of the dirt and either (a) dusted off or (b) not, depending on the level of sadism present in your trainer, scoffed at or outright laughed at, possibly rewarded with a small smile and nod, possibly applauded for your ability to withstand whatever horrors your equine has chosen to present you with today. And this whole experience has cost you an amount of money that would feed a small village in Africa for an entire week.

But it is worth it because, baby, you are *on,* spot *on*, not a centimeter to the left, not a centimeter to the right, but *on, on, on* the Golden Pathway. And it feels great.

The Golden Pathway is a glittering place, not at all dissimilar in appearance to the fabled Yellow Brick Road. A happy, shiny place, the Golden Pathway is that point at the end of the lesson when you have accomplished the objectives of your lesson and you and your trainer are reveling in the fact that you "made it all work." You leave the lesson, bathed in the Golden Light and with your horse's hooves glittering with Golden Dust from the Golden Pathway. The world is good, sweet and harmonious.

The Golden Pathway is different for ever rider. If you are a relatively advanced dressage rider, the Golden Pathway might be the perfect canter pirouette. If you are someone like me, it might be

---

[4] Just be sure that you have a few spare hours of your life that you are just begging to never see again. And I personally recommend not executing this particular move unless heavily sedated.

four steps of quality trot that are steady with the $700 Pony quietly accepting contact. But the point is, the Golden Pathway is where you are when you leave your lesson and all is right with the world.

The very next day, the very next time you set foot in that stirrup, you begin the journey *off* the Golden Pathway. You hop up on your steed, still glowing and shiny from your lesson the previous day, and you wipe a spot of Golden Pathway Golden Dust from your fingertips and set off. But your trainer is not there, and it doesn't take long before the Golden Pathway Golden Dust wafts off behind you in a murky cloud.

Suddenly, instead of following your trainer's barking commands, you are trying to remember those barking commands—and execute them. But you are not a trainer. And remember the Jell-O analogy? Increasing barometric pressure when you really need to add sugar makes the Jell-O just turn out, well, wrong. With your horse partner, it's not like random application of barking commands will get you anywhere. You might be remembering "left leg, left leg, harder, now!" at a moment when the command the trainer would be barking if she could see you would be "Sit UP! Sit UP! Sit UP!"

And so you slide off the path. It's just a little bit at first—and less if you are actually rider with a modicum of talent or retention. But if you are like most of the adult amateurs I know, you start your post-lesson ride all glittery thinking, "I've got it *now!*" And by the end of your ride, you are rooting around for your cell phone to see if your trainer could possibly fit you in sooner then next Wednesday.

Any more questions? Please see diagram above right.

When the trainer/therapist saw the $700 Pony for the first time, we were so far off the Golden Pathway we might as well have been in the Emerald City. If I *could* actually have been there and petitioned that wonderful Wizard of Oz, a brain for me, a heart for the $700 Pony and some courage for the trainer/therapist would have been in order.

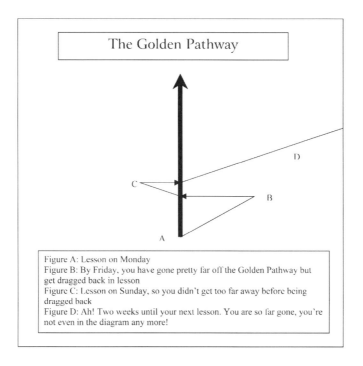

The Golden Pathway

Figure A: Lesson on Monday
Figure B: By Friday, you have gone pretty far off the Golden Pathway but get dragged back in lesson
Figure C: Lesson on Sunday, so you didn't get too far away before being dragged back
Figure D: Ah! Two weeks until your next lesson. You are so far gone, you're not even in the diagram any more!

But I have known the trainer/therapist for many long years and she takes pity on me. So she lassoed us in and dragged us, kicking and screaming, as close to the Golden Pathway as she could given that she only had half an hour.

The trainer/therapist began the lesson brightly in that loud, deliberate voice that makes me wonder if she thinks that my IQ and hat size are within striking distance: "*So*, things are not looking so good here, are they?" And it was in that bright, measured voice that she began distributing her Golden Nuggets—millions upon billions of Golden Nuggets, all designed to get the $700 Pony and I on track—to the entrance of the Golden Pathway.

She started with a few basic suggestions, like, maybe I should try a full cheek instead of an eggbutt bit. Maybe I should start riding in my dressage saddle instead of the Stübben. Maybe I should try a standing martingale. Oh, and if I slowed my posting down, what would happen? And, *honey*, what are you doing with your hands there? Can we *please* stop that *right now* and *never do it again, ever, for any reason?* And, "My goodness, taking Two Children off has not really helped your riding at all, has it?" And so on. For half an hour. I am sure you can relate.

But at the end of half an hour, the Pony and I had our marching orders. The $700 Pony was a pretty long way from being sold to finance my PT Cruiser dream, but every long journey starts with a few small steps. Probably the best thing was that by the end of the lesson, the trainer/therapist had warmed up to the $700 Pony—at least, a little bit. While she was not impressed by the $700 Pony's gaits, submission, impulsion, obedience or charming personality, the trainer/therapist did turn to me as I was shaking the Golden Dust off my hands preparing to head home and said, "You know, she really does have a lovely tail."

CHAPTER 7

The $700 Pony Gets a Trace Clip

There are so many wonderful things that we can learn from the repository of all knowledge we so lovingly call the World Wide Web. How to properly clip a pony is not one of them. Well, perhaps it's not so much that the *knowledge* isn't there. I mean, the textbook stuff is available, the technical, how-to can be printed out, read and re-read, and there are even photos! The *theory* behind a successful trace clip is readily available. Like many things in life, however, the successful clipping of a pony is not about theory. It is pretty much all in the execution.

I had an extra half an hour the other day, so I trace clipped the $700 Pony. Bells are going off, aren't they? I know, you are thinking, "Girlfriend, *half an hour*?" And logically, even I have to admit that there's no way that could work. I mean, for example, the area of my head is only, what, half a foot by half a foot square, give or take a few inches? And yet I pay someone a small fortune to waste a good 45 minutes of my life to clip me. The $700 Pony, while only a pony receiving a partial clip, represents a significantly larger surface area than the 36 squares inches, give or take, of my skull.

So what in the heck kind of trace clip can you give a pony in half an hour? Well, the short answer is not a very good one. For the long answer, keep reading.

Basically, this chapter of the $700 Pony's life reads pretty much like all the others. Let's start with; the only time I can get out to the barn is either pre-dawn or post-48-orphan-puppy-equivalent's bed-time. Early, late—either one is tragic. I have been putting off trace clipping the Pony because (a) I suspect it will take longer than the few minutes I ever have to spare, (b) I suspect I will do a pretty crappy job and I am going to embarrass both myself and the $700 Pony, and (c) because I just hate the way those clipped hairs get under your clothes and make you itch for the next decade.

But there I am, one freezing cold night, at, oh, about 10 pm, thinking, it's now or never. While it is true that I will shrivel up and die if I am not in bed by 11 pm, it is also true that if I don't clip this blessed critter, she is going to start shedding her winter coat and it will be too late.

But it was with some trepidation that I approached the $700 Pony's first clipping. And you might be asking yourself, "Hey! How do you know that Pony has never been clipped?" Come on. I bought a completely green pony from a ramshackle barn. You think she had ever been clipped before? Yeah, and I believe that one day she will sit down while on the lunge line and start reciting her ABCs.

I do believe that deep inside the Pony there is a kind soul. She has not had an easy life, so sometimes her kindness manifests itself in ways that you might not traditionally define as "kind." She has not, thus far, graced me with any kind of flesh wound, although not so much for want of trying. It's more that, despite my advancing age, I have thus far been faster than she. She has demonstrated other traits that belie her true, kind inner self, I think. But that said, given that she is, as has been previously pointed out, the evil triumvirate—chestnut, pony, and mare—she, all in all, is pretty reasonably behaved.

So, bracing myself, I grabbed the clipper, wasted about four minutes of my precious half an hour reading the directions, plugged the puppy in and went at 'er.

And now time for a quick multiple choice test: I, of course, ever the consummate professional, have taken careful time and attention to acclimate her to a clipper by (a) clipping her face, (b) clipping her ears, (c) clipping her bridle path or (d) *thinking* about doing all of the above but never actually getting around to it. Anyone answering a, b or c, please go back and read chapters 1-6 and try again. The thing had never seen clippers.

So I turned on the clippers. And because deep inside she is such a *nice* pony, the kind of weird alien from another planet *nice* chestnut mare pony that I never imagined existed before, she does not take a chunk of flesh. She does not try to kick me. She does not try to break free and run for the hills. No. The deep-inside nice Pony *faints*. And I don't mean she behaves like some kind of equine drama queen, throwing herself to the ground in a fit of vexation. It is more like she sucks in her breath, her eyes quietly roll back into her pony skull and with a grace and aplomb rarely seen in the equine world, and she slips to the ground in a dead faint.

May the heavens strike me dead if I am lying.

With no smelling salts in the immediate vicinity (oh, *darn*, what a time to leave my smelling salts at home!) I grabbed the can of kerosene I was using to, well, whatever the heck it is you do with that stuff when you are clipping, and splashed a little under her nose. Her eyes fluttered open, and she raised her head delicately from the soft bricks of the grooming stall.

As she came to, you could just see the thought bubble forming over her head, "Now what in the heck happened here?"

While I helped her to her feet, I explained to her inner-kind-pony self that she needed to please keep breathing when I next approached her with the clippers.

I started the clippers again, and you can just repeat the above five paragraphs in their entirety. Twice.

With time ticking away and my brain threatening to turn into a pumpkin at the ridiculous lateness, I decided that a little negotiation was in order. I indicated the few random patches of hair I had managed to clip out prior to her repeated losses of consciousness and suggested that her friends out on the pony playground were going to tease her something awful if I didn't finish what I started.

Then I showed her the really cute gigantic purple Wug blanket I had struggled for weeks to purchase. For the amount of time and effort that went into getting that pony a Wug, I could have flown Jean-Paul Gaultier over from Paris and had him sew a blanket for her. But I digress.

The point is, I appealed to her better nature and finally did, in fact, manage to convince her to continue breathing while I clipped. Unfortunately, I was down to only a few conscious minutes awake myself and finished the job in what can only be described as a "hurried" manner.

She looked OK when I was done. A little tufty here and there, and I really left most of the fur on her underbelly (it gets *cold* out there on the pony playground and a little belly fur is probably a positive thing), and in the dark light of the grooming stall, she looked like there was some kind of zebra-stripe thing going on with the clipper lines. But I was pretty sure she'd look better in the light of day, so I slipped on her brand-spanking-new, practically-made-to-order Rambo Wug and headed home to get a good night's sleep.

The next day was Saturday, and I was actually able to get out during daylight hours. That turned out not to be such a great thing. Sadly, there were lots of people around when the $700 Pony's new trace clip was revealed.

Unfortunately, my reputation with the FSF people is not all that good. First off, most days I arrive at the barn at 5:30 am, and while I did ascertain prior to moving the Pony to the FSF that they wouldn't mind if I rode early in the morning, I suspect that they were probably just being polite when they said 5:30 am would be fine. I mean, surely they did not think that I would really show up every morning that early to disturb their quiet, peaceful start to the day? I now suspect that they suffer quiet regret when I roar into the driveway, headlights glaring into their bedroom hours before reasonable people are expected to get up.

I am also one of those snail-like people, which is not to say that I am slow, so much as I leave a trail behind me wherever I go. Not a slimy one, which is good, but a trail, nonetheless. It might surprise you, having gotten this far through this tome, that I am not ultimately the most organized human on the face of the planet. No, it doesn't? Ah, well, just be glad you are not in my daily orbit.

But I do tend to leave my things all over their very nice barn. One day, it's my jacket, another, my helmet. One day I left the Pony's bridle hanging on the hook in the grooming stall, another I forgot to put my cooler back in my tack trunk. Let's put it this way: Even if they manage to sleep through my headlights, they always know when I have been by. At first, they kindly picked up my stuff and left it lying on my tack trunk. But nowadays, I tend to find my discarded belongings right where I left them, often looking sad and forlorn, awaiting my return.

And then there was the day they caught me riding in front of the trailer. That is one of those sentences that make absolutely no sense without context. And with context, well, it's pretty embarrassing. Here's the back story: the FSF for all of its fancy-schmancyness does not have mirrors in the indoor. For someone who has spent her entire adult life riding in front of mirrors in eventing and dressage barns, the idea that you would spend a fortune putting up an indoor and then not put up mirrors so you could watch yourself tormenting whatever sorry equine you happened to be tormenting that

day seemed kind of dysfunctional. But as I have mentioned, the FSF is a hunter/jumper barn and it appears that segment of the horse world does not use mirrors! You learn something new every day.

But while the FSF people do not have mirrors in their indoor, they do have a really cool super-duper, long, bright, shiny, flashy aluminum-skin trailer. The thing is gorgeous and, like just about everything at the FSF is kept in premium tip-top condition. I swear the thing looks like someone periodically spends half a day polishing it. Very lovely. And just like a big, honking, mirror. You can probably guess where this is going, right?

One day, the aluminum skin trailer was parked in front of the barn, and, as you might expect for a very long, heavy thing on wheels, on a lovely flat place. The sun was just peeking over the horizon giving the world that lovely pinkish early morning glow. The trailer was just calling my name. Yes, I decided to ride in front of it like it was a mirror. Unfortunately, it happened to be a morning when the FSF people were up and about particularly early. I was practicing upward transitions on the driveway in front of the trailer when I happened to glance up and there they were: the FSF contingent watching with, I swear, their jaws on the ground. They just never know what I am going to do next.

With that kind of background, it would have been in my best interests to keep the Pony's trace clip under wraps until it grew out. But I didn't. I was there to ride, and it's not like I could go away and come back later when they were gone. My meager window for riding was open, and I either had to peel off her blanket in front of the crowd or leave. So I peeled.

The 8-year-old granddaughter of the barn owner, who already knows more about horses than I will know in my lifetime, stopped dead in her tracks when I removed the blanket. The child's eyes were rolling so far back in her head I was afraid she was having a seizure. But no, she was just expressing her interest in something she, as she put it, "had never seen before!"

Given that the $700 Pony was in a fancy-schmancy *hunter* barn, I did think it was possible that the young lady had never seen a *trace* clip before, as everything within eyesight looked like it had been waxed, stem to stern.

No, she shook her head vehemently, "*Of course* I know what a *trace* clip looks like," she cried. "But I have never, ever, *ever* seen a clip like, like, like (she pointed a shaking finger at the poor beleaguered Pony), like *that* before!"

I was appropriately chagrined and embarrassed, not only for me who was responsible for this clipping travesty, but for the poor, innocent Pony. Turning a flaming shade of red, I ducked my head, mumbled something about the eventing world being *totally* different from the hunter/jumper world and got the heck out of Dodge as quick as I could.

The good news, I suppose, is that the Pony is much happier working without the burden of her trace hair. She sweated a good deal less and was much more comfortable and looks quite dapper and sporting in her Wug. Sadly, though, we are the laughing stocks of the barn.

And perhaps the unkindest, saddest cut of all? I tried to sneak the trace clip past my trainer/therapist without mentioning it. Not possible. It was a bit like dying your hair a ferocious shade of pink and just hoping no one will notice. When I walked the $700 Pony into her indoor at my next lesson, my trainer/therapist stopped dead in her tracks and whistled a low, sad whistle. "Girlfriend," she asked, "do they *laugh* at you at your barn?"

Yes, honey, they sure do.

CHAPTER 8

Wild Kingdom Runs Amuck

And so the winter passed. I got to the trainer/therapists fairly infrequently, so the time the $700 Pony and I spent together on the Golden Pathway was relatively brief. Inevitably, I would have some minor epiphany while riding in a lesson, leave covered in the magic Golden Dust, but within 24 hours, be back pretty much at square one, struggling with the combination of one very green pony and one out-of-shape, not-very-talented rider.

But I did have fun. I am nothing if not an optimist, and while I can look back on the winter and wonder if our time might have been better spent if somehow I had found more time to ride with the trainer/therapist, the reality is that I did not. And so we went on. We did the best we could, entertained ourselves mightily and dreamed of competing in the spring. Or at least, I did.

As spring slowly edged her way to our part of the world, the $700 Pony and I began venturing outside together. While I have to say that we had a whole passel of issues that we needed to work on inside, there were a whole new set of obstacles that reared their ugly heads outside.

To be truthful, despite my stated desire to event the Pony, I am not the bravest rider outside the indoor ring, which, if you know anything about eventing, is kind of bizarre. While I am being truthful, I should point out that I am not the bravest rider *inside* the indoor ring, either, but outdoors, well, I am basically fairly cautious.

And like most cautious horsepeople, my cautiousness stems from some real-life experiences—you know the kind of stuff that you just don't ever tell your mother about because she would forbid you from ever going near a horse again, despite the fact that you are 40 years old and have not lived at home for 20 years.

For example, in the fine state of New Jersey, there has been some development in recent years. It gets harder and harder for horsepeople to find great outdoor places to ride. In most instances, you are required to ride your fine equine on the road in some way, shape or form in order to find hills and dales on which to ride.

I don't much like riding on the road. Most people don't mind it so much I believe. But I am just not a fan of it and generally just won't do it, mostly because I have been hit by cars too many times in my life to *not* get nervous every time a car passes. I suppose I am *lucky* as I am one of those people who has been hit by cars multiple times and survived to tell the tales. I consider myself fairly lucky, actually, as I do keep rebounding for more. But maybe I am *unlucky* as I do seem to find myself in the path of a speeding vehicle more often than the average human. Or maybe just really, really clumsy?

Ah, well, whatever. But luckily, only one of my run-ins of the vehicular type has actually occurred while I was on horseback. And while it does not concern the $700 Pony much beyond explaining in part why I find riding on the road so abhorrent, it is a rather interesting tale. And so I shall tell it.

Lo, a few years ago, my Sport Utility Horse (SUH) and I were hacking along a quiet dirt road in the fine state of New Jersey. SUH was a fairly quiet beast. As his job description at this juncture in his life was "pet horse" and he was a right good one at that, he had been basically somnambulant for the previous five years. He sometimes startled to life during thunderstorms, but it took about that much.

SUH and I had walked down the same little dirt road four times a week for the past five or so years. We had walked past the same small farm with a white picket fence and a passel of hysterically vocal Jack Russells. For five years he had not blinked. And then one day, there was a paradigm shift. On that lovely afternoon, one that seemed no different from any other afternoon, as we were passing the howling pack, an SUV of the variety that would allow you to carry heavy artillery if you were so inclined also happened to be passing in the opposite direction. The planets were in an unfortunate alignment. As the artillery carrier passed, the dogs barked and the SUH woke up. Shocked to find himself outside (we assume he thinks all exterior activity is some kind of overactive dream state), SUH swung his butt to the left and connected solidly with the door of the SUV. Thunk.

The SUV driver pulled over as I hopped off. The damage was clearly severe. To the SUV, I mean. While SUH looked mildly startled at best, the driver of the SUV was unable to open his door.

Crawling out the passenger side door, the shell-shocked driver called out, "That is the first time I have ever been hit by a horse!" Un-shell shocked and recognizing that I might be in a somewhat vulnerable position legally, I retorted, "And that is the first time my horse has been hit by a car. Shall we contact the local law enforcement agency?"

Our local officer of the law was called to the scene of the crime. Officer Joe is third- or fourth-generation lawman in our small town. With a few beers in him, he claims to have seen it all. This, he had never seen before. Horses get hit by cars, almost always to the detriment of the horse, oftentimes to the detriment of the car, but Officer Joe had never seen a car hit by a horse where the horse was still standing and the car was a TKO.

Officer Joe took our statements (mine and the SUV driver's— SUH was munching grass and the instigator Jack Russells were off tormenting local wildlife) and informed me that he needed all of my personal information, including a way to get in contact with me that night just in case he needed to issue me a summons. Mind you, I have known Officer Joe since he was a geek in Chess Club back in high school.

Me: "A *what*?!"

Officer Joe: "A summons."

Me: "A summons for *what*?!"

Well, Officer Joe volunteered, in the state of New Jersey, a horse is technically a motor vehicle and, as such, I was negligent in my management of said motor vehicle and so could be held responsible for any number of motor-vehicle-type violations.

SUH a motor vehicle? Officer Joe looked at SUH, now dozing under a maple. "No Ferrari, that one, huh?"

I happened to be one of the few nonlawyers in the neighborhood I lived in then, so after spending a few minutes with the vet to ensure that SUH was as undamaged as he appeared to be (indeed, undamaged), I hurried home and made a few phone calls. Sure enough, in the fine state of New Jersey, SUH is covered under motor vehicle law, and with a high degree of probability I was going to be responsible for the damage to the SUV.

Now, SUH was insured for major medical and mortality, but not liability. I called his insurance company first, just for the sake of covering all bases. Turns out, if he had died, I could have collected the pitiful amount he was worth and forked it all over to SUV Man to pay for the damages. No such luck.

Next, I called my car insurance company. Heck, if SUH was technically a motor vehicle, why wouldn't he be covered by my car insurance? Not surprisingly, they laughed like hyenas, but could not help me.

Next stop was my home owners' insurance. Except for one niggling detail: at the time of the SUV-SUH collision, I was living with my then fiancee. We were planning to be married shortly; however, at the time of the accident, we had not yet tied the knot. While his casa may have been my casa in spirit, technically, I was a "tenant" in "our" home, and I would not be covered under "our" homeowners policy until "we" utter those magic little words "I do" and the state conferred on us the formal status of a couple. (Additionally, as further research turned up, for those of you who may find yourselves in a similar situation, many homeowners' policies specifically exclude equines.)

And sure enough, SUV man's insurance company called me and demanded I pay for the damage to the car. Luckily, I am blond and was able to use that to my advantage. I cleverly asked them to please have their lawyer write me a letter stating the legal reasons that I needed to pay for the damage, which is the adult equivalent of a 4-year-old human putting her hands on her hips, sticking out her lower lip and saying in a very loud 4-year-old voice, *"Make me!"*

Which, if you think about it, is probably the smartest thing I could have done. I never said I *wouldn't* pay. I just said they needed to have a lawyer tell me that I needed to pay. Once I injected the magical, very pricy word "lawyer" into the discussion, they rolled over and gave up.

There were some long-term repercussions from the event. SUH and I ended up in the police blotter of our weekly town paper, which basically turned us into local celebrities. I got probably a hundred phone calls from people asking me if I was OK. Funny how you never think about who reads the police blotter.[5] Well, I now know who reads it: basically everyone.

Truthfully, the event took a psychological toll. I am quite loathe to ride the $700 Pony or any horse for that matter anywhere near macadam. Despite the flippant tone of the above story, it is darn *scary* to be hit by a car, on or off a horse. And since SUH was the equine critter on the planet that prior to the accident I would have voted "Least Likely To Do Something Really Stupid in Traffic," the accident really made me gun-shy.

And for those of you who have a great familiarity with horses, you know they are basically psychic when it comes to stuff like this. If you are afraid, they are afraid. It is a herd mentality thing, and frankly held them in pretty good stead when they lived wild on the

---

[5] I would also like to point out that recently I was quoted in *Businessweek* magazine. While I got a hundred phone calls after showing up in the police blotter, how many calls do you think I got from people who noticed that I was quoted in a major national publication? Would you have guessed none? Yes, exactly none. So, there you have it. You want small town fame and fortune? Get mentioned in your local police blotter.

plains of wherever horses actually lived wild and were preyed on daily by things that would hunt them down and kill them.

So I chose not to ride the $700 Pony anywhere near the road. I mean, the thing was practically paralyzed with fear just walking around outside the barn, so taking her out near the road where my fear plus her fear would result in an escalating fear that was sure to be significantly more than the sum of its parts was just a bad idea.

Luckily for me, the FSF did have several hundred contiguous acres within which we were able to roam. I have to say that when it did start to get warm enough for me to start riding the Pony out of doors, I was kind of looking forward to it. I mean, Bob had described her life prior to entering mine as one full of trail rides with small children. Rationally, given the Pony's level of training and her general behavior, it didn't make sense that any halfway caring parent would let her child within a 100 yards of the critter, but I was willing to buy the story, probably because I'm not always the sharpest tool in the shed, myself.

Our forays in the wilderness, which began as soon as the weather and morning light allowed, ultimately resulted in my acceptance that Bob had probably massaged the truth a bit on the "trail riding" thing. The Pony was not well acclimated to things like grass, shadows, wind, trees, rocks or other naturally occurring substances that you would think she would have had at least some degree of comfort with had she spent any time in the great out of doors.

But there are so many stories, so little time. Where, oh, where should I start? In an effort to move this saga along, I will limit myself to two tales that fall under the category of Wild Kingdom Run Amuck.

The horse, a four-footed, 1,000-plus pound animal, is ill equipped to deal with predators. The horse has no claws to speak of, lacks protective shielding and possesses teeth that are not all that useful for defensive action. Flight is the horse's primary and singularly most effective response to most predator-encountering situations. The good news is that most American equines no longer encounter naturally occurring predators. The bad news is that they have not yet figured that out.

Instinct, or "directives" for those who are politically correct and in tune with current bio-theory, cause our precious beasties to worry that every rock, every shadow, every snapping twig is either a mountain lion about to spring upon their vulnerable backs or a wolf about to lunge out and snap their hamstrings. And as these things were reality not so long ago, it is hard to argue that horses should give up their instincts. I mean, it took millions of years for those instincts to evolve, who are we to say that they should give them up just because, for this century, wolves have been eradicated from the state of New Jersey?

But horses come in many shapes, sizes and brain types. The $700 Pony is a bit of a throwback. While there are some breeds that are relatively quiet and have evolved quite a bit toward understanding the realities of modern living, the Pony would not be among them.

While, in general, the $700 Pony tries to please, she apparently had not had much exposure to the bright city lights prior to her time with me. Certainly there are some who would argue that at least she had not been ruined by bad riding. I would argue that while she didn't know much, everything she did know was wrong. And as for exposure to some of the harsher realities of life in the big city, well, the girl was as green as my spring pastures. Dogs made her heart pound, blowing dust clouds caused her to lose her cool and the mere sight of my trailer would cause her to hold her breath, bringing her perilously close to a dead faint.

And while many, many ordinary things (like garbage cans, for example, or a newspaper lying on the grass, or her reflection in an indoor mirror) frighten the $700 Pony near to death, two categories spring to the forefront as catastrophic: things-that-*might*-be-mountain-lions and things-that-*might*-be-wolves. Things-that-might-be-wolves are categorized based on my belief that she believes that they will snap at her hamstrings. Things-that-might-be-mountain-lions are things that are more likely to come down from above.

For example, dogs are clearly things-that-*might*-be-wolves. This makes sense even to me, the nondirective driven human that I am. Dogs do look an awful lot like wolves and when those tragically low-to-the-ground hounds that haunt the FSF come roaring toward us in a billowing cloud of fur and dust the collective hearts of myself and the $700 Pony skip a beat.

However, the fact that the $700 Pony apparently views squirrels as mini-mountain-lions-with-long-furry-tails causes me some degree of consternation. Yes, they live in the trees above us and rustle and make a dreadful bit of noise. And while I personally view the squirrel as a suburban rat, the fact that it causes the $700 Pony to lose her grip on reality is an issue.

In fact, the list of things that might be predators, according to the $700 Pony, contains some pretty far-fetched links to predation. Most of them are not even carnivores. For example, geese are two-legged white mountain lions that say "honk, honk, honk," and bunny rabbits are skittery, tiny but potentially deadly wolves. Sheep and pigs are a little easier: woolly wolves and stinky wolves, respectively. Pheasants in any language are unidentified flying objects.

But these are the proverbial small fish in a vast ocean compared to the mighty big fat slow wolves that say "moo." How on earth you could ever imagine a cow gathering enough speed to catch a flighty little pony is beyond me, let alone thinking that this huge lumbering beast could make a concerted run at your hamstrings. But the Pony is the Pony and thus it is. The $700 Pony discovered cows and her fear of them early one bright spring morning.

We were out hacking on aforementioned early spring morning when, in a previously empty field, I spied two rather unimpressive bovines representing someone's farmland assessment project. For those of you living in a fine agricultural state like New Jersey, you are probably well versed in the ins and outs of farmland assessment. For those of you in less agricultural regions, I'll provide a short primer.

In the fine agricultural state of New Jersey, we have a law that allows people who possess more than five acres of land to farm it and claim a lower tax rate based on agricultural land value. To qualify for this fine tax break, you have to generate revenue at a level appropriate to the amount of farmland you possess. For the baseline five acres, you have to generate $500 in revenue. For people like me and my husband who have 130 acres and a multitude of agricultural products, it's not hard to generate the required revenue. But for some, the baseline $500 can represent quite a hurdle.

Which translates into some creative farming. Christmas trees are a big one for people with relatively small "farms" and not a lot of farming expertise. Basically, you plant them and get credit for farming for a bunch of years while they grow with the assumption that you will harvest the trees at some point and generate the requisite revenue. This works really well as long as you actually take care of the trees and keep the deer away. It's a little harder if you plant 'em, ignore 'em for half a decade and then come around to harvest and there's nothing left but the little toothpick stumps the deer so kindly left behind.

I have a few friends, for example, who make their farm living selling sheep. Their original intention was to raise sheep to eat. They purchased feeder lambs in the spring with the idea that the little lambs would keep the weeds down, give the place an appropriately genteel, countrified look and then fill the freezer full of fresh lamb meat in the fall. Yum!

Unfortunately, the best-laid plans of mice and men are often interrupted by wee children. When time came to process the lambs, the children threw their young bodies in front of the pasture gate. Wailing that they would become vegetarians if the darling lambs ended up in the freezer, the children refused to let the parents by, and said parents quailed. But what were they to do?! If they did not in some way make use of these sheep, they would fail to fulfill their farming obligation and thus lose their tax relief!

So they sold them. The sheep that is, not the children. You might wonder how they could bear to part with them. Well, they didn't exactly. They sold them to their next door neighbors, who, as it turns out, were in much the same boat. They had also purchased feeder lambs in the spring that turned into pet lambs over the summer and were most definitely not going to make the leap to freezer lambs for the winter.

So, neighbor #1 sold his feeder/pet lambs to neighbor #2. And neighbor #2 sold his feeder/pet lambs to neighbor #1. The next year, they sold 'em all back. And the cycle went on for the life of the feeder lambs—and the lives of the next round of feeder lambs. Nice gig for the lambs, for sure. And while perhaps not fully vested in the spirit of the farmland assessment tax relief, they were technically selling sheep each year and so were in compliance with the letter of the law.

But the neighbors with the bovines were a little more vested in the farming spirit. They were the type who bought feeder calves every spring and saw them through to the freezer in the fall. This year's crop of bovines, and let's call them Roy and Roger just to add a little flavor to this story, were idling about their pasture as bovines are wont to do. They were quietly minding their own business as we ambled past. At least we were ambling until the $700 Pony caught sight of R&R. Then we weren't ambling anymore. In fact, all forward momentum ceased, the $700 Pony broke out in a violent sweat, and her little heart tried to make a break for home on its own.

I was perched atop $700 worth of quivering, near-hysterical equine, brought figuratively to her knees by a pair of cows. Not being much of an equine psychologist, I suggested to her that she might want to think about continuing our amble without showing much regard for her fears. When she did not respond, I increased the level of "suggestion" and shortly thereafter we found ourselves in a heap in a ditch. Deciding that a little equine psychology could go a long way, I returned home to elicit advice from horse friends wiser and more well versed than I, which would include just about every horseperson on the planet, including the 8-year-old granddaughter of my barn owner.

The proposed solution was theoretically brilliant; the $700 Pony spends her days turned out in the pony playground with a slew of

other ponies from the FSF. While most of the ponies looked down their fancy little sculpted noses at the $700 Pony, she does have a best pony pal. This pony was actually a former cow pony from out west. She was a 30-year-old behemoth affectionately and respectfully known as Mrs. CP. She had been known simply as "Cow Pony" before her arrival at the FSF, but her venerable age, her gentle good nature, plus her affinity for pushing around the younger stock in a motherly sort of way, had earned her the honorific "Mrs." before the acronymic "CP."

Mrs. CP was as out of place at the FSF as the $700 Pony herself, which is perhaps why they bonded. Turning their noses up at the $70,000 hunter ponies (who snickered at the idea of anyone turning their noses up at them), the $700 Pony and Mrs. CP would while away the hours chatting over flakes of hay and generally trying not to overhear the other ponies muttering to themselves about how the neighborhood had just gone to heck in a Longaberger basket.

Mrs. CP belonged to a lovely older gent who would pop out every few weeks, saddle up his ancient former cow pony and head out to the hills for a little gentle loping. They were a lovely pair. He was a horseman of old and when he discovered that the $700 Pony was having difficulty with bovines, he shook his grizzled head at such equine silliness and suggested that I enlist the trustworthy and far superior Mrs. CP to fix the $700 Pony's wagon.

Since she had a known affinity for bovines, the suggestion was to ride Mrs. CP down to cow territory with the $700 Pony in tow. Mrs. CP would stare down the bovines and transmit her lack of fear to the $700 Pony. The $700 Pony would in turn realize how silly her fears were and the cows would formally cease to be an issue.

Now "in tow" for those of you who just reread that paragraph trying to understand what in the heck I could possibly be talking about, is a technique formally known as "ponying." Extra points to anyone reading this who actually knew that the word "pony" can be a verb.

Yes, "pony" is a verb. It is the act of riding one horse while holding on, via a lead rope, to another one (or sometimes two more, for the very brave or very stupid). In some racing circles (and I know this to be true because I have seen it done) people will sit on the back of a pickup truck and hold three or even four lead ropes while the horses trail on behind. This is a way to get a large number of horses exercised quickly. Thinking respectively about the laws of gravity, motion and thermodynamics, I would no more execute a move like this than I would jump out of a plane without a parachute, but we all have our own fear thresholds.

But I would consider ponying one horse, especially since I would be ponying one small pony from the broad, stable and sensible back of a slightly larger pony who used to live with cows. And the two horses were best friends? Icing on the cupcake!

Awestruck by the elegance of the solution, I made a date with the owner of Mrs. CP. I did grill him a bit. Yes, she is 30 years old. Yes, she lived most of her life before her retirement to the FSF with cows. Yes, she worked cows for almost 25 years. No, the owner of Mrs. CP had never fallen off of her. Yes, he had ponied tons of horses from her sensible back and she would be fine with it.

So feeling quite in the cat-bird seat, I tacked up Mrs. CP, strapped on the standard bag-o-treats to feed the happy pair once

Mrs. CP transmitted her lack-o-fear and with visions of sugar-coated bovines dancing in my head, trotted off on Mrs. CP with the $700 Pony in tow to face the bovine marauders. For those of you with a literary bent, Robert Burns should be coming to mind right about now.

I do believe that the plan would have succeeded if I'd had the foresight to clue Roy and Roger in. It hadn't occurred to me that they might have an alternate plan. They had been so quiet and cow-like during our previous visit. They were considerably less cow-like this time around.

As the $700 Pony, Mrs. CP and I turned around the bend in the field that would take us past the bovine pasture, we were struck by a sight I have never seen before and hope in all my riding days never to encounter again. Roy and Roger were, well, for want of a better word, *playing*. I have never seen cows play before, but these two were be-bopping up and down the fence line, bucking, rearing spinning and generally participating in some very uncowlike behaviors.

Mrs. CP took one look at these two idiot creatures and the decades melted away. The $700 Pony decided that a return to the pseudo womb was in order, slammed herself up against me and Mrs. CP and stuck there like we were lashed together with Velcro. Mrs. CP was "transmitting" to the $700 Pony alright—*"RUN, RUN, RUN!"*

The three of us—two clearly terrorized equines and one dim-witted human—began a bizarre *pas de trois*, passaging and piaffing with the occasional air above the ground thrown in for my amusement, as the Mrs. CP/$700 Pony unit struggled to escape the clearly deranged bovines. R&R were thrilled with the attention and only redoubled their unbovine-like activities.

Now stuck with 2,000 pounds of terrified equine, the jaunty air with which this sojourn had commenced gone and the pitiful bag-o-treats useless and forgotten, I decided that discretion was my friend. High tailing it for home, almost a mile passed before the $700 Pony was able to unstick herself from her surrogate mother and my leg. And as I tried in vain to return circulation to my squashed limb, I vowed to significantly increase my intake of red meat, the better to seek revenge on the cavorting Roy and Roger.

The epilogue to the story is short and sweet. Roy and Roger are no longer with us, having joined that great cattle drive in the sky— or the great freezer in the basement. Whatever. But they remain firmly entrenched in the $700 Pony's razor-sharp brain. As she passages past their empty paddock in a state of high equine hysteria, I just sigh and try to comfort myself with the thought that if I ever want her to passage on purpose, I may have to invest in my very own big, fat, slow wolf that says "moo."

That was the cow story. And now for the deer story, which, frankly, is even weirder.

Despite all evidence I have presented to the contrary, I believe the $700 Pony is quite a clever little creature. Her wicked habits, nasty quirks and the general suspicious ill will she exhibited toward me are for the most part signs of a rather normal, well adjusted mare. Mare, of course, being the operative noun.

As the cycle goes, mares are the bearers, nuturerers and protectors of baby horses. Baby horses are the natural prey of all manner of predator. So, in order that the species continue, Mother Nature wisely equipped mares to protect their babies.

Consequently, mares are tough as nails, ever wary and quick to react to changes in their environment (that is, blowing leaves, the occasional downed tree limb, sunrise; you know, strange, unnatural occurrences). Good baby-protector mechanisms, albeit a poor skill set for human/equine interaction.

In addition to being ever alert to any and all changes in her environment, the $700 Pony is prone to react rather negatively to the presence of deer. When I was younger and less horse savvy, I accused horses spooking at deer of stupidity. "Deer," I would yell, clinging like a drunken monkey to some long equine neck, one leg over the saddle, "Deer are not going to eat you! Deer are stupid, flighty little things—dumber than you even!"

But ever wiser as I am now, I recognize, of course, that the $700 Pony was not afraid of deer. Silly me, deer are Mother Nature's early warning system. Deer are even more yummy than baby horses, so their flight mechanisms are highly sensitive. If they weren't, there wouldn't be any deer.

So when the $700 Pony takes flight at the sight of a small herd of deer skittering across a field, it has nothing to do with any concern she may have that the *deer* will eat her or her future young ones. Her concern is that there might be something chasing the deer that will have culinary designs on her. Or so I suppose. It sure beats thinking my horse is dumber than dirt.

What follows is a strange and out-of-character deer story that really has nothing to do at all with the above paragraphs, other than that they all contain the word "deer."

Once upon a time, early in the spring season, the $700 Pony and I were casually sauntering down a local dirt road. We were "casually sauntering" and not "working" due to an emotional scene involving a very minor sliced heel and a drama queen equine whose tolerance for pain is nonexistent.

On the buckle we strolled, drinking in the spring-like air of late March, with the just-rising sun at our backs. Ah, if life could be so grand all the time! But we were not alone.

Rounding a bend, we normally passed a small field that has, on occasion, hosted a herd of likely-to-flee deer. In a typical episode of Wild Kingdom Run Amok, they will spy the $700 Pony, flag their tails and run. She will spy them running, flag her tail and run. I will curse roundly, disturbing all creatures great and small within 150 yards. Just a typical morning in our rural neck of the woods.

This lovely morning, we happened on the first ever sighted herd of New Jersey Rogue Deer.

Now, we reside in a fairly bucolic locale, a place one generally does not anticipate much gangland activity. New York, L.A., Chicago, yes. Rural New Jersey, no. But, nonetheless, on this morning, the $700 Pony and I encountered what can only be described as a street corner gang of juvenile delinquent deer. Oxymoronic, perhaps, but true.

There were at least eight little guys; six looked to be just barely yearlings and two were older instigator types, leading the yearlings astray. Squinting in the morning sun, I could just imagine them wearing little black leather jackets with chains, a couple of nose rings on each mossy snout, puffing away on their Camels, and generally terrorizing the forest geriatric set

As the $700 Pony and I chanced on the scene, the two older JDs were teasing the little ones, poking them with their noses, chasing them around the field and generally provoking what looked to be a rather wild game of tag. The *"You're it!"* part was particularly fascinating. It turns out that deer make little bleating sounds that I would previously have called "goatlike," though now that I know better, I will refer to as "deerlike." Who knew?

The little ones were giddy (with the sun up and all, it was clearly way past their bedtime, and, who knows, perhaps there had been some underage imbibing?), and the melee churned on, with older deer poking the younger ones, the younger ones running off bleating, then spinning around and dashing back for another poke. It went on for quite a bit without the little beasts realizing they were being watched.

And watched they were. I don't know who was more fascinated, me or the $700 Pony. She stood on her little tippy toes, eyes bugged out, snorting quietly to herself. I did much the same, wishing I had a video camera to capture the moment for posterity.

When the little devils finally noticed they were being watched, the yearlings froze. You could tell they were embarrassed to be caught behaving so inappropriately so far past their bedtimes.

The older boys, however, knew who had the upper hoof. They had probably encountered the $700 Pony running away from them at some point in their lives and, with a gleam in their eyes, decided to show the little ones a fun new game.

Heads held high, nose rings gleaming in the sun, older deer one and two turned their attention away from the youngsters and came trotting straight at me and the $700 Pony bleating like, well, like deer.

The yearlings, caught in the spell of forest delinquency, popped their little heads in the air, joined in the chorus of bleating and single file trotted after their older partners in crime. Just a reminder, by the way, this is a true story.

No need to describe the $700 Pony's reaction in graphic detail. She flew backward as fast as she could, backed her fancy blond tail into a fence and stood on tiptoes, pushing back against said fence with all of her might, snorting in abject equine terror.

Can you blame her? I was pretty taken aback by the attack of the rogue deer myself.

The good news is that her reaction brought the little juvies back to reality. Remember, deer are easily alarmed, and the sight of one terrified equine breathing brimstone and fire froze them in their tracks.

In that frozen moment the $700 Pony saw her exit. With blinding speed, she leapt off the fence and fled down the road. The rogue deer, once again sensing the upper hoof, regrouped and, still in single file, came galloping right after us, bleating to beat the band.

While deer are usually fleet of foot, the night of partying had apparently taken its toll on the young gang. We left them in the dust as we pounded down the road, breathing a huge sigh of relief that we had escaped the clutches of the New Jersey Rogue Deer.

In retrospect, I'm not sure what the little fellows would have done had they caught us. Perhaps all they wanted to do was give her a poke with their noses and have her join in their game of tag. All I know is that the $700 Pony and I sure haven't looked at deer the same since.

CHAPTER 9

We Interrupt The Regularly Scheduled Program to Bring You A Primer on Equine Sports

We will shortly be entering the phase of the $700 Pony's life wherein I decide it is time to compete her in public. It will be abundantly clear at the end of those chapters that this is an idea before its time. But at this point, who knows that? And so it seems to make sense here to provide a little background on what I mean by "compete."

If you are not a horseperson, you might have the impression that all horsepeople are basically alike. Maybe a little snooty, if you have the image in your mind of someone wearing tall black books and a pair of tight-fitting stretch pants. Or maybe rugged and a little rough around the edges, if the word "horse" puts you more in mind of the Marlboro Man. But if you are a horseperson, you know that term "horseperson" can mean many different things. And if you are not, the above example may at least have you thinking along that track.

But a discussion of the diversity of equine sports here in the United States could go on for days. We could start by breaking it down to English versus Western, which are terms most people, horseman or not, are familiar with. You know, little postage-stamp saddle versus big saddle with a horn to hang on to. But that simple breakdown misses a whole slew of horse folk: two that come immediately to mind are Driving People (those who ride behind horses in carts) and Racing People (definitely not Western, but does being not "Western" automatically make it English?).

Driving People can drive Roadster Ponies, or American Saddlebreds or Morgans or Fjords, or they can be Combined Driving People, or they can be Pleasure Driving People. And Racing, well, that can be flat racing (horses that run with people on their backs) versus harness racing (back to those people riding in carts again) versus Steeplechase (horses that run over jumps). And flat racing people include Thoroughbred Racing People and Quarter Horse Racing People, to name just two. And none of the above include the Halter People (people who show horses like dogs—on a leash).

Halter people show Miniature Horses and Non-miniature horses (oh, wait, let me think about that for a minute now—a non-miniature horse would be a *horse*, wouldn't it?) all sorted tidily by breed: Arabians, sport horses, Quarter Horses and more! And really, where do you fit polo and polocross? Or endurance riders? We haven't even started on the breakdown of people who ride English. If you ride "English," you might do hunters, jumpers, eventing, dressage, or saddleseat. Western riders can do reining or cutting or pleasure

or, well, even ride as a mode of transportation if they work on a cattle ranch. I really could go on for days, and it could make your head explode just thinking about it.

Just try to explain this stuff to people who only know horses as "big smelly things that eat grass." Say some poor, uninformed relative by marriage who really just wants to make small talk at a high-school graduation party asks, "So, I hear you have a horse. Do you ride English or Western?" Where do you start?

From my perspective, I generally start with, "Well, I don't have a horse, I have a pony." And while that does not make a whit of difference to Great Aunt Helen twice removed (or my husband who always insists I am bandying semantics when I insist that I have a pony and not a horse), I have to say that I would never tell a horseperson that I have a horse. I mean, if they took one look at her, they would realize she is a pony and call me out as a great big liar, liar, breeches on fire.

And do I ride English or Western? Well, definitely not Western. That's easy enough. But I don't race or play polo or ride jumpers or hunters. I do a little dressage, although mostly so I can jump. But wait, if you jump, doesn't that mean you do jumpers? No, no! I jump so I can gallop cross-country, and yes, technically stadium jumping is part of my sport, but it's not the same!

So, now that I have completely muddied the waters, let me take a few minutes to explore the arenas, literally, within which I compete.

My sport of choice is something currently called eventing. I say "currently" because there are movements afoot to change the name. Mostly because from a marketing perspective, "eventing" is kind of a hard sell. It goes something like this:

"So, Ellen, what are you doing this weekend?" asks a non-horseperson friend.

"Well, I'm taking the Pony to her first event!"

"Oh, what kind of an event?"

"Well, an *event*. Pleasant Hollow's having their spring event!!

Other person looks puzzled. "But what do you mean? What KIND of an event?"

The sport also goes by, or maybe used to go by (I can never keep up with all of the changes) "combined training." Combined training actually makes some sense if you know that the sport of "eventing" consists of three phases. The three phases are as follows: dressage (which is its own sport and will be explored in great depth later), cross-country (which is not its own sport) and show jumping (which, similar to dressage, is its own sport). There has also been some talk recently of renaming the sport "Horse Triathlon" in an effort to bring eventing to the masses—to which I say, are you kidding?

Reflecting the constantly changing nomenclature, the U.S. Combined Training Association (USCTA), of which I am a member, in the last few years, changed its name to U.S. Eventing Association (USEA). Shame they didn't think of the "Horse Triathlon" thing sooner, because then they could have been USHoTA, which would have been much easier to remember than USEA. Particularly given that that event (by which I mean the event of the name change, that is not the event of an actual event, like Pleasant Hollow, see example above) coincided with the American Horse Shows Association (AHSA) changing its name to the U.S. Equestrian Federation (USEF), which should not be confused with the U.S. Equestrian Team (USET), who has not yet mentioned making a name change, but I am sure would like to just to stay current with the rest of the herd.

So, back to the original purpose of this chapter, which is to elucidate the sports I compete in. As mentioned above, eventing is a three-phase sport consisting of a dressage test, a cross-country jumping round and then a stadium jumping round. I'll start by explaining each of the phases individually before addressing how they all link together.

The art of dressage is classical, beautiful and, when done correctly, poetry on horseback. I, of course, am not poetry on horseback. I am more like some tragically twisted nursery rhyme bonking along in the saddle:

Hickory Dickory Dock,
Look, she fell on her block!
The horse he run, down she come,
Hickory Dickory Dock!

Dressage as a training platform is all about the logical progression from simple to increasingly more difficult movements (by the horse, as directed by the rider). The act of learning these movements teaches a horse to be obedient, willing, supple and responsive, again, if done correctly.

Dressage as a competitive sport consists of a series of increasingly more difficult "tests" that are scored on a movement-by-movement basis. If you can remember way back to when figure skating actually had a figures phase, it's the same concept. You ride a prescribed test with every movement given a score from one to 10, which are all added up at the bottom with coefficients given for really hard movements and a total score is awarded.

At the Olympic level, dressage is a sight to behold. Huge, gorgeous extravagant-moving horses, polished and gleaming to reflect the sun, enter the hushed arena ridden by a quiet, lovely, well-groomed individual wearing a perfectly tailored shadbelly,[6] formal dress boots burnished to a high sheen, glowing white breeches and a silk top hat. This is the attire you would chose to wear around a 1,500 pound animal whose main job in life is to slobber and poop, is it not?

The Olympic rider quietly and confidently guides his or her mount through the incredibly difficult Grand Prix test while the

---

[6] A specialized formal riding coat with tails. It is found in the sport of dressage and the dressage phase of eventing at the higher levels and specialized hunter classes. I do not own one. I will never own one. I will never compete at a high enough level to warrant one, which is good, because they cost way more than my $700 Pony.

hushed crowd watches silently. It is truly poetry as the aids the rider uses are virtually invisible, and the horse seemingly responds to telepathy.

But I sure don't ride at the Olympic level—or even close.

At the most basic level of dressage, Training Level, the rider must demonstrate the incredibly simple basics of halt, walk, trot and canter circling in both directions. By Grand Prix, levels and levels later, the pair can execute a "circle" at the canter without the horse ever moving the hind legs from one spot (technically called a pirouette) along with a whole host of other movements that all have fancy French names. It's a lot like ballet, I suppose, only done outdoors.

The difference between Training Level and Grand Prix is a bit like the difference between the Boy Scouts Pinewood Derby and Formula One auto racing. For another perspective, think of the sport of dressage as a little like the task of teaching a young child to read. Training Level is a comprehensive knowledge of the ABCs. The child can sing the song, including the bit about "singing with me," and can recognize by sight each letter of the alphabet. First Level, the child begins to read whole words: cat, dog. Second Level, the child is reading about Dick, Jane and Spot, assuming children still read about those nice folks. Third Level, child has progressed to chapter books and Fourth, Stephen King.

We kick it up a notch when we get to the upper levels: Prix St Georges, the child is now reading and comprehending Faulkner, Fitzgerald and Hemingway. Intermedaire I and II, add classic Russian authors like Chekhov or Doesteyevski. And Grand Prix? Well now our child protégé can read *War and Peace*—in the original Russian. It generally takes years for really talented people with really great, athletic horses to make this progression. So there is basically no hope for the $700 Pony and me.

Dressage is judged subjectively, which provides all kinds of room for infighting in the horse world. A test consists of a series of movements executed by each rider at each level and then judged.

The number and complexity of movements increases dramatically through the levels. At Training Level (Test 1), there are 13 movements, the most complex of which is "halt." By Grand Prix, you are executing 32 movements, half of which are unpronounceable French things that would require way more time than I have to describe. Let's just say they are really, really hard and leave it at that.

And not only is each *movement* in a dressage test scored, but the horse is given overall impression scores in three areas: "gaits" (does the horse have a nice way of walking, trotting and cantering), "impulsion," (did the horse demonstrate sufficient get up and go) and "submission" (was he or she a good boy or girl horse). And then, horror or horrors, the *rider* gets a score. Only one. Only one rider score that determines if you are basically an impediment to your fine steed who is plunking along bravely despite you, which would be a score of 4 or 5, (and, yes, I have gotten both at one time or another); OK, you don't suck totally, but you're not very helpful either, which would be a score of 6; or good job which earns a 7 or 8 (and, yes, I have gotten both at one time or another).

Individual scores for all the movements are added up divided by some coefficient or other and a percentage out of 100 is calculated. So what would you think a "good" dressage test score is? Would you guess 95%? Maybe 85%–90%? No, not even close!

In fact, a "good" dressage test is one that breaks 60%. No kidding! A score that would have failed you in high school chemistry (and come to think of it, I did fail high school chemistry) is considered a "good" score. A great score is anything that breaks 65, and a really great score is in the low 70s. Yup, most of the Olympic riders when they are competing for the glory of their country get 70s, which would have been a passing grade in high school chemistry, but a "C" for sure.

So where do I fit in on the dressage hierarchy? I have ridden, albeit not terribly well, at First Level, which as I explained earlier, translates to Dick and Jane on horseback. Tragic, is it not, particularly since I have been riding for more than 30 years? But not unusual. Horses are nuanced and I, along with many of my fellow dressage-challenged compatriots, am not.

And the Pony? Well, she is so new to riding that we as a pair do not even qualify for Training Level. What, you say? There is something *below* Training Level? Yes, indeed! For those who are truly dressage-challenged, there is something called "Intro." Intro dressage tests are walk and trot tests! You don't even have to *canter!*

Well, that was a pretty long explanation for something that represents only the first third of eventing. Remember eventing? The sport I say I compete in? Eventing begins with a dressage test. The horse, or in our case, the $700 Pony, must demonstrate for a judge that she can execute a simple dressage test. The eventing dressage tests are put together by the USEA[7], so they are a little different from the tests that USDF[8] and FEI[9] put out, but are based on all the same principles.

The interesting problem with all of this is that the real point of eventing is in the running and jumping. Many people who event have a tiny bit of disdain for the dressage phase. I mean, you have to do it because it is required, and people who can do it well as well as run and jump tend to be pretty successful. But if you really, really in your heart-of-hearts love dressage, well, why wouldn't you just compete in dressage? So, for many eventers, dressage is the phase to be borne so that you are allowed to go blasting around the cross-country course, which brings us to the second phase in eventing.

The second phase in the sport of eventing, called cross-country is really the heart of the sport. Dressage and show jumping are stuff

---

[7] That would be the U.S. Eventing Association, remember?

[8] U.S. Dressage Federation—you knew there had to be one, right? They only create the Intro A and B Tests. Training through Fourth Level tests are put together by the USEF (U.S. Equestrian Federation). The FEI tests—Prix St. Georges thru Grand Prix are put together by the FEI. See below.

[9] FEI is the International Federation for Equestrian Sports. Which you might think would be IFES, but FEI is *French* for International Federation for Equestrian Sports. FEI is the international governing body for all equestrian Olympic sports.

other people do. Cross-country is for eventers! Well, there are hunter paces and people who fox hunt do something that is kind of like cross-country, only they do it in groups and, well, maybe it's not worth getting into here. I think I've made the point that the horse world is a crazy place, full of weirdly overlapping and yet incredibly divergent type sports.

But in the cross-country phase of eventing you basically run around a preset course (on horseback of course) of relatively natural jumps. These jumps are typically made of lumber, telephone poles, rock walls, and stuff that does not come down if you hit it (which predisposes the horses to not hit them) and may vaguely resemble something that might have been put there to serve some purpose other than to leap over it—like a pile of split wood, a pheasant feeder, or a chicken coop. Courses also include trick stuff designed to freak out the horse, like water, up and down banks and ditches, and even something called a "coffin." A coffin usually consists of a vertical fence, followed a stride or so later by a ditch followed a stride or so later by another vertical fence. Lore holds it that it is called a "coffin" because horses are likely to bury their riders in the middle ditch. Nice sport, huh?

All in all, when things are going well and you have a horse or pony that likes to go cross-country, it is a hoot and a holler. You gallop around really fast (but not too fast because you are being timed and you get penalty points if you go too slow *or* too fast!) and jump over cool stuff! This is all great, unless the horse or pony in question decides that his or her life's work is not, in fact, to seek out scary, immobile objects to leap boldly over with some moron *yahooing* on his back. Some horses are smarter than others.

Penalties are awarded based on the different things that might happen at a fence. For example, if you run up to the fence and the horse decides that discretion is the better part of valor and swerves to avoid the obstacle (which, I should point out is what 99.9% of horses in the wild would actually do if faced with such a decision), you are awarded penalty points. If you do that three times, you are eliminated. Also, if the horse falls down or you fall off twice, you're eliminated. And that's about it. I mean there really are only three options: (a) you go over it, (b) you don't go over it or (c) you fall down in some way attempting to go over it.

You can tell a lot about this part of the sport from the way we dress. The conservative black coat is replaced by a safety vest, designed to help cushion ribs and reduce incidence of rib breakage and overall bruising when you accidentally flip your horse over one of those immovable objects. Remember Newton's First Law of Motion? An object at rest remains at rest and an object in motion remains in motion? The fence remains at rest, the horse flips in motion and the vest cushions the blow of the hard ground, which is most certainly at rest when you arrive in motion. Nice sport, huh?

But cross-country is the part of the sport most eventers live and breathe for. It is a roller coaster-ride thrill, particularly as you climb the levels and begin jumping fences that you can't see over from the ground.

Having survived cross-country, the final test of our equine tri-athlete is stadium jumping. This test closely mimics the sport of show jumping, which is a jumping sport featuring brightly colored fences made of relatively lightweight airy poles that fall down if your horse accidentally hits them. This makes for a much safer jumping course, but one in which penalties are awarded for things like knocking down a rail. Again, if your horse swerves to avoid the fence and you have to re-present, you are awarded penalties, but the most likely thing to happen is that you knock bits of the fence down (which in my mind is so much nicer than flipping over the fence) and you are penalized.

There are all kinds of levels for show jumping, too, and like dressage it is its own Olympic sport, but if you get the basic principle that the fences are brightly colored and fall down when you hit them, you've got the gist of it.

And there you have it—the three phases of eventing! Sounds like oodles of fun, doesn't it? Ah, but wait, there's more!

The sport of eventing, much like dressage also has levels. The most basic level recognized by the USEA is called "Beginner Novice," followed by Novice, Training, Preliminary, Intermediate and Advanced. There are all sorts of complications that go with the higher levels, but these levels are so stratospherically out of my league that they are not worth even discussing here. Let's put it this way: the only way I will ever go to the Olympics will be if I buy a ticket.

It is of interest to note that in this sport you have three levels present before you get to the one called "Preliminary." Sadly this seems to be part of the dumbing down of the sport for people like me. What we call "Preliminary" in this country is actually called "Novice" in England. To put it in perspective, Preliminary fences are maximum of 3 feet, 7 inches, which is pretty big if you are powering down to a fence that you know is not going to move if you flip over it. Beginner Novice is 2 feet, 7 inches, which can look pretty big from the back of a $700 Pony.

And so the plan that formed in my mind, lo those many months ago when I made the fateful decision to purchase the $700 Pony, was that I would turn her into a lovely little eventing pony for some lucky child. Knowing that there is a relatively small market for equines thusly trained, I never did suppose that I would make a bucket of money on her.

But I did think that I would be able to bring her up the Golden Pathway fairly quickly and perhaps get her out competing in the spring, and probably have a lovely eventing season with her, taking her thither and yon, perhaps qualifying for the year-end championships or some other such thing that would probably increase her value—at least enough that I would be able to contribute something to the eventual PT Cruiser that would take her place.

Reality, however, was moving slower than my dreams. Truly, the Pony had been greener than green when I bought her, and the three years I had taken off from riding were proving to be no benefit. The Pony at this stage of the game was not ready for an event. Not even close. But starting at an event as your first competition is generally not a good idea. You want to start by getting your feet wet at a few dressage shows to acclimate to the "show environment," a hunter show here or there to get them used to the idea that stadium jumping is a sound notion, and cross-country schools are mandatory so that they have a chance to acclimate to the idea that they should actually leap over things that, in their natural environment, they would simply run around.

And thusly, like a fine wine consumed perhaps before its time, the show career of the $700 Pony began.

CHAPTER 10

The $700 Pony Begins Rolling and Gathers No Moss, Part I: The Hunter Show

Showing is a lot like riding a bicycle, by which I mean, at a certain point in your life, you probably should just stop—like when you get to the point when as fast as you can pedal, you are still being overtaken by a 3-year-old.

And yet, there is something about competition that is so compelling: the thrill of hitching up the trailer, getting your finely tuned and spiffed-up equine out in public, wearing your fancy show clothes, not to mention the satisfaction of hanging up all those ribbons so your friends and neighbors can ooh and aah at you.

Although at this point in the Pony's riding career, she wasn't really ready to hit the big time—or even the little time. But I have a friend, who, for the sake of argument and anonymity, we'll just call the "The Instigator." I will say that The Instigator is the "go-to" woman in my area. If you have a question about anything, and I do mean anything from architecture to zebra-striped polos, The Instigator can point you in the right direction. It just so happens that she also has two wee children who are close in age to my two wee children, so I go to her for child as well as equine care advice.

The Pony's show career was launched at the suggestion of The Instigator. She called one day and announced that she was taking her children to the local horse park to a show and that there were classes that were perfectly well suited for a $700 pony. I could feel the immediate adrenaline rush.

The show The Instigator was going to was a hunter show. These shows are usually referred to as hunter/jumper shows because they have hunter classes as well as show jumping, which as I mentioned in a prior chapter, is fairly similar to the stadium jumping phase of eventing. This particular hunter show, though, did not have any jumper classes and actually had some Western stuff as well as the lead line and showmanship classes The Instigator's children would be contesting. It was an interesting mix of stuff but nothing really for the Pony if I were planning to "compete" in the true sense of the word.

The Pony would not, in any way, shape or form, be competitive with the hunter-type people. She does not look like a hunter-type pony and she does not jump like a hunter-type pony. And while these differences might be subtle to the uneducated observer, they are not if you are a participant in the sport.

In addition to the Pony not looking or jumping like a hunter pony, hunter people *ride* differently, *dress* differently and use different saddles and bridles than eventing people. Again, these things are so subtle as to be nearly undetectable to the uneducated, but are rather serious and glaring to the well schooled.

If the Pony were better schooled and I got a hold of a different color jacket (the hunter people frown on black whereas the dressage and eventing people *only* wear black or dark navy) I might blend in a little better, but the point of entering this show was not to compete against the hunter people. The point was for the Pony to jump around a few courses, all of which would be good prep work for getting her to an actual event. Basically, she would not be in a position to actually win a class or even be third or fourth, unless of course there were only two or three other horses in the class with her.

However, since all I really wanted to do was to let her jump around some courses and start *thinking* like she was an event horse who could, with relative ease and nonchalance, pop around a random assortment of jumps in a ring, the hunter show was the perfect opportunity for me. And so began the planning phase of the Pony's hunter career.

As you may know by now, planning is my forte, but execution is my downfall.

The planning was relatively simple. I had not been to a horse show of any sort for a good four years. Much like riding a bicycle, I assumed that it would all come back to me. And it did in little tiny data bits at random, assorted times, usually when I was least prepared to do anything about it.

For example, I own a glorious pair of custom riding boots. They were perhaps a bit more glorious 15 years ago when I first had them made for me, but despite their rather ratty current appearance, they are still my pride and joy. I suffered for those boots. Fifteen years ago, they cost more than twice my monthly rent—more, in fact, than I paid for the Pony. That makes for a whole heap of pennies. So I ate Ramen noodles for months on end, washed out my own work clothes in the sink to save on dry-cleaning bills and, in general, lived as much a life of parsimony and cheapness as a 23-year-old living in Manhattan can (which is to say that my entertainment bill was reduced, although not zeroed out, in favor of actual food purchases). But a pair of custom boots was mine!

When the boots were done, well, they fit like the proverbial glove. So snug, in fact, that they cut off my circulation and, made me feel woozily claustrophobic. But that is the price we pay for the highest style and fashion! A bit of wearing and they did expand somewhat. By the time I went to my first competition in them, I looked so forward to slipping them on! They felt featherweight, like I was wearing angel wings on my feet.

Now the boots were 15 years old, and as I had given up riding while on broodmare duty and moved a couple of times, the boots had been consigned to the attic. I was a little afraid to bring them down. Bearing children does many nasty things to one's body, increasing the size of feet being one of them, and the size of everything else being another. While most of my clothes still fit pretty well, there are enough qualifiers in that last sentence to make me shudder at the horrible thought that my boots, my precious, custom, hand-made-only-for-me-at-a-price-that-makes-my-head-spin-just-thinking-about-it, might possibly not fit.

At the first call from The Instigator that a showin' we would go, I ran up to the attic and brought my boots down. To my unmitigated horror, they were *dirty!* I don't mean dusty or bat guano speckled from being in the attic. I mean, *dirty*—covered with whatever I had last stepped in, around and on when I had last worn them those many years ago, pre-two wee children.

The point in bringing them down from the attic was to try them on to make sure they still fit. My horror at their condition, though, made me do exactly what I can well imagine any other concerned person would do when seeing the deplorable condition of her favorite possessions: I threw them in the back of my closet and promptly forgot about them.

My other show clothes were also of questionable ilk. Remember, my clothes are going to stick out at a hunter show no matter what. Hunter riders have riding "fashions" that change with the times. Dressage and eventing riders are generally much less fashion conscious, so old clothing tends to work just fine. For example, hunter riders went through a phase many years ago when they wore rust-colored breeches. They are now considered an abomination. The color currently in favor? Well, it's lovingly referred to as "puke green." Go figure. Dressage people wear white breeches and eventing people wear either white (if they are very brave) or tan.

Hunter riders also wear multicolored shirts under their jackets, such as green, purple or pink, all in more pastel rather than vibrant shades. However, they also like designs and stripes to run through their shirts. Many, many years ago, they used to wear chokers around their necks that had little pins in them. Now the chokers all have monograms or "bling" on them. Dressage and eventing riders wear a formal stock tie called a cravat that is tied properly with a square knot and secured with a stock pin, a style that has not changed since German dressage Olympian Reiner Klimke was a pup.

My show clothes were going to stand out, but, I continued to rationalize it all by reminding myself that I was not really competing. I was only using this competition as a way to school the Pony, so, I would be dead last no matter what, and the right clothes, the right tack and the right saddle pads weren't going to change that one way or another.

I dug out the rest of my show clothes. Breeches: tan. Check. Riding shirt: white. Check. Choker tie: white. Check. Jacket: black. Check.

And my breeches still fit! I knew this because my show breeches and my everyday breeches are technically one and the same. Hey, whatever, at least they fit. And, the *piece de resistance*, the thing that made me feel a little less bad about the tragic condition of my hand-made custom boots, was that my show jacket was actually wrapped up in dry cleaner plastic, as though I had actually had it dry cleaned before I put it away! I had not taken it out for a few years, but frankly figured that since all of the rest of my fitted jackets fit post-pregnancy, that this was a no-brainer and I should devote that millisecond of my spare time to more worthwhile projects.

Sadly, there were no belts were to be found. It is hard to explain the importance of a belt. There is something tidy and correct about a nice pair of breeches, a tucked in shirt and a belt, so I try to wear them to all of my lessons and clinics (the operative word here being *try*). So a belt is important, but mine were all missing. I had looked at a few on my last trip to the local tack shop, but I wasn't in the mood to spend $30 on a belt. Now some of you might be wondering why I would pass up something as inexpensive as $30. For others of a more of a $700 pony mindset, a trip to Wal-Mart was in order.

Now with two wee children, a trip to Wal-Mart, known affectionately in my family as Warmit (rhymes with "varmit" and is the best pronunciation The Elder can come up with), is not to be taken lightly. It requires significant advance planning (around feeding and nap times) as well as during a time when Warmit will not be crowded or the lines too hard to get through.

With great advance planning, we made the sojourn early one summer morning. I did make a quick stop in the ladies department thinking that perhaps there would be a tasteful, skinny, black belt that would suit my purposes. Shockingly enough, the Warmit version of high fashion does not include skinny black belts for ladies. Rather all they had were colors and styles that frankly would not suit my purpose, unless my purpose was planning for Halloween.

But I am not one to be deterred when I'm on a mission, and I had a Plan B. Off we headed to the boy's department. And here is my fashion tip for all of you not-too-tall and not-too-wide ladies out there: If you need a cheap, simple belt, hit the Warmit boy's department! Two belts for $5! One black and one brown—perfect!

And thus I was outfitted for my re-entry into the world of showing. I hustled all of my show clothes into bags and boxes, and with the exception of my boots, loaded it all into the trailer. The plan was to arrive at the show in a pair of shorts, get the Pony cleaned and tacked up and then change into my show clothes. The boots, of course, remained in the bottom of the closet because they need to be (a) cleaned and (b) tried on.

The next critical issue was the care and management of my wee children. My mother was coerced into a visit and because she dearly loves my wee children and also dearly loves me, and always rises to the occasion when I cry for help. She agreed to take three days out of her life, spend a chunk of change in gas and be bossed around by me for the duration, all so that I could spend a few minutes piloting the Pony around a hunter course.

The day of the show dawned bright and clear. I had given a lot of thought as to how much time and energy I was going to put into getting the Pony ready. There is a lot you can do, and the Hunter people by nature tend to go whole hog. Bathing is a basic first step, followed by clipping all errant bits of muzzle, facial and leg hair, followed by braiding the mane and finally braiding the tail. As this was a very small local show, I did not expect to see any braided tails, although I assumed I would see some, if not all, manes braided. And then, generally, clean tack is a basic minimum requirement.

I made the executive decision that my tack would be clean, the Pony would be clean, I would be clean and that would be it. I was going in to this with a clear understanding that we were not on any kind of competitive footing with the other riders at the show, so anything more would have been overkill. Any less, of course, would have been disrespectful, and I certainly did not want to be disrespectful. Quite the contrary: I wanted to be as respectful as possible, since I was going to stand out like a sore thumb anyway.

And so it was easy enough to get out on time. As shocking as that may seem, I simply got up early, took a shower, gave the Pony a quick bath, wiped off my tack and headed out. It was almost too simple. I felt a little bereft, as though the adrenaline rush that usually accompanied any journey I made was missing. And I felt a little sad that it had gone astray.

Oh, there was a flurry, here and there. The realization that I had never actually tried on my boots hit me as I was sneaking down the back staircase at 5 am. But I realized it soon enough to grab my boot bag and shove it and a cleaning kit in the trailer.

The cleaning of tack post shower proved to be a bad idea. My tack was filthy and by the time I had gotten it clean enough to be presentable, the dirt that had ended up on me cancelled out my shower. But it's not as though the judges ask you to take off your gloves and check your fingernails for cleanliness, so I wasn't really worried. And the strategy of *not* putting on show clothes was a good one. That was a lesson I had learned the hard way years and years ago. Put on show clothes at the last possible second! So while my shorts and t-shirt were filthy with dirty tack and dirty Pony stuff, my show clothes were safe and snug in the trailer.

And the advent of wee children into my life had brought one huge bonus: the discovery of baby wipes! How did I ever survive without these little godsends? Put a pack of those puppies in your truck and all yuckiness can be tamed!

So it was with a touch of smugness that I pulled into the horse park and got a lovely parking spot. I sat in my truck watching with quiet satisfaction as the show scene came alive around me. Unfortunately, the show grounds were not the only thing that came alive at that moment. Do you ever suffer from earworms?

You know what an earworm is, don't you? It is that little bit of a tune that pops into your head, runs through whatever bit you know of it and then hits rewind—*ad nauseam*? My earworms seem to have lives of their own. Part of it comes from having children. I find myself singing to them quite a bit, so an earworm can develop and come to life as I begin humming it aloud in an endless loop, and it becomes entertainment for them.

An earworm can be anything. Seemingly one of my favorites, although having a "favorite" earworm is a little like having a favorite hangnail, is the Eagle's "Life's Been Good." I know this is a favorite earworm because I'll unconsciously hum it and my two-year-old human will start warbling the words, "My Maserati does one-eighty-five! I lost my license and now I don't drive!" Unfortunately, that would be about the extent of my familiarity with the song, and thusly, his familiarity with the words. He and I will hit rewind and repeat the same lyric fragment over and over again. Luckily, my children have a very sane, well-grounded father to balance me out.

I don't know how you would have felt at this moment, if it were your first horse show in four years, but I was a bit on the nervous side. It wasn't so much competition nerves, as we all know that I was not competing, but I was presenting the Pony in public. If I were being at all truthful with myself, which is something I am not very good at, I would have admitted that she really didn't belong here today, so I was a little bit nervous. We all have different strategies for dealing with nervousness. Some people eat, some people nibble on their nails, and some people throw up, although I'm not really sure that is technically a "strategy."

But it seems one way I deal with nervousness is to hatch an earworm. And on this bright morning as I sat watching the show grounds come to life, an earworm was born and migrated to my vocal cords. If my children had been with me, they would have alerted me to the earworm developing. But I was *sans* children this particular day, and one of the really odd things about this particular nervous habit is that it happens completely unbeknownst to me. Can you imagine just sitting around, humming out loud and having no clue that you are doing such a thing? Well, I still suppose earworms are a better strategy for dealing with nerves then throwing up, but probably not by much.

The grounds were getting busier, and The Instigator arrived with her two darling children and their adorable pony. They were doing the lead line division so they would be riding at around the same time I was, but in a different ring. This was a good thing, as I was not excited by the prospect of having The Instigator actually see me ride. I had been having some serious doubts about how well the Pony was going and was feeling pretty amateurish.

I reminded myself that I was there to jump, and, again, if I were being at all truthful, the Pony was not really ready to be jumping. I mean, I had started the process, but I was having trouble getting to the trainer/therapist's as regularly as I should. And I would have to say that as far as jumping was concerned, we were nowhere near the Golden Pathway. The $700 Pony's general philosophy toward jumping was pretty similar to her approach toward life in general: when in doubt, go faster! She had a tendency when I was jumping to be a bit, well, *quick*.

But there's not a lot of time in my life for reflection, thank goodness, so I shook off the creeping doubts and headed off to register for my two classes. Now I have to confess what classes I have gone to all of this trouble to *not* compete in. I was planning to jump

(1) a course of four two-foot fences and

(2) a course of six (bring on the hard stuff, baby!) two-foot fences.

Those of you who know anything about this stuff at all have just fallen off of your chairs and are doing everything in your power to keep from peeing yourselves laughing. Those of you not in the know, well, let's just say that to go to all of this trouble to jump what turns out to be a grand total of 10 two-foot fences in front of a judge who is going to take one look at me and the Pony and throw away her judge's card is, well, laughable. In fact, I would say that it is fall-on-the-floor-and-pee-yourself laughable.

But the whole point of this grand adventure was to get out and jump a couple of courses, which I could probably have done at my neighbor's house if I had just picked up the phone and asked her. However, there is something about competition, about being at a horse show, about wearing the clothes (even if they aren't quite the right clothes) that is, I don't know, so heady and powerful. In this case, it was all in the spirit of getting ready for a real competition although in the cold light of day, I was so far away from being ready for a real competition, that I was a little embarrassed. But I am waxing philosophical here, and I think we have agreed that I don't really have time for that kind of crap in my life.

So where were we?

Ah, yes. I entered my two classes and I headed back to the trailer to get the Pony ready. The Pony was watchfully alert to her new surroundings. She was clearly put upon by the proximity of other horses and trailers. In fact, she was particularly put upon by the rather large, boisterous woman who had chosen to park right next to us. I tied the Pony to the trailer while I groomed her and tacked her up, a rather standard practice and one she is pretty good at, thank goodness, and had her just about ready to go when Boisterous Woman noticed her.

Now, the Pony looked pretty spiffy. Her spectacular blond tail had been beautifully fluffed and combed. Her pretty chestnut coat was flat and sleek. Her tack was gleaming. In general, she looked pretty darn, well, pretty. Boisterous Woman boomed over.

"NICE HORSE YA GOT THARE! GOOD SIZED ONE, TOO!"

I was a little taken aback by this comment as the Pony is clearly a pony, not a horse. And while she is a solidly built 14-hand pony, the "good-sized-horse" comment didn't really ring true. But I thanked Boisterous Woman for her kind words and kept on with my pony prep. Then Boisterous Woman opened the side trailer door and I was enlightened.

Out popped the cutest, tiniest little horse head you can imagine! Boisterous Woman was a Miniature Horse Person!

This is going to be hard to explain for the uninitiated, so please bear with me. As most of you probably know, in general, a horse is any equine over 14.2 hands, or 58 inches tall. Ponies are those equines that fall short of the 14.2-hand mark—except for Miniature Horses.

A *Miniature* Horse is a horse that is not a pony, although it is technically short enough, at 34 inches or less, to qualify as "pony sized" based on the above definition. They are a breed apart and are bred, apparently, from real horses who happen to be very tiny, versus ponies, thus the confusing nomenclature. Or something like that. The point is a Miniature Horse is a teeny, tiny horse. Not to be confused with a pony. If that is not clear, it is because I am not really clear, but if you talk to a Miniature Horse person, whatever you do, don't call their Miniature Horse a pony. It ticks them off.

So there was Boisterous Woman, with her very own petite equine, who, in fact, appeared to actually weigh *less* than she did! Her

Miniature Horse was a sparkly, happy-go-lucky little fellow who looked like as though a stiff wind might blow him down, while it would clearly take a Category 5 force storm to mow down Boisterous Woman.

So naturally Boisterous Woman took the $700 Pony to be a good sized horse! Just about anything equine next to her sprightly little fellow would be! BW then pulled out all of these cute little purple and pink brushes and cleaning implements. It was like a little Barbie® Doll horse set! And then, and I swear if I did not see this with my own eyes I would not have believed it, she *lifted* her little pony out of the trailer like one of those tiny dogs all the Hollywood people drag around! She set Tinkerbelle, er, maybe Tinkerboy in this case, gently on the ground, tied him up and began her own preshow cleaning routine.

The Pony looked askance at this tiny equine, her eyes bugged out and she snorted quietly and shook her blond mane almost as if to say, "And now I have seen *everything!*" But show time was upon us. The Pony looked shiny, bright and clean, and it was time for me to put on my fancy show duds. Standing in the trailer with the $700 Pony tied up outside, I put on my spiffy, clean tan breeches and my clean, white shirt and reached around for my boot pulls to pull on my—shoot! Boots! *Boots*? Shoot, I forgot about my boots!!

Alarmed, I ripped open the boot bag and the guano-encrusted, dirty-from-years-ago boots stared dully out at me. Darn it, they were such nice boots! And now they looked like they had been left hanging out dirty in an attic for years, which, of course, they had.

Since I had remembered to jam my boot cleaning kit in my bag on the way out, I set to work restoring them. First I scrubbed the years of dirt and grime and heaven only knows what else off, then I slathered them with boot polish, you know, that indelible stuff that really makes them shine. Then I buffed them carefully with a lovely horsehair brush made just for this purpose, and then I carefully finished them with a finishing cloth. It was a miracle! The boots looked unbelievable!

And the best part was that with a handy pair of boot pulls, I pulled them on and, miracle of miracles, they actually still fit! I could feel a little bit of pull against my small toe, but they fit my calves as though I were still the same size I had been 15 years ago! My hands were slathered with indelible boot polish, of course, but with the judicious use of baby wipes and gloves, no one would be the wiser.

I was unable to bask in the glow of my success for more than a millisecond, because just as I pulled my boots on and was admiring my own quite spiffed up reflection in their glowing selves, a fight broke out at the trailer next door—between Boisterous Woman and the Miniature Horse!

I caught the first round out of the corner of my eye, and although I am not quite sure what words were exchanged that might have instigated it (perhaps Tinkerboy made some snide comment about the size of the fringe on BW's black suede attire?), Tinkerboy *leapt* into the air and *swatted* Boisterous Woman! Yes, I saw this with my own eyes! Boisterous Woman, not one to take that kind of behavior lying down, swatted him back! And the fight was on! Boisterous Woman got the crap knocked out of her at first, but Miniature Horse Tinkerboy had less stamina! She eventually got him into a half nelson and overpowered him!

I will say I was pretty impressed with the example these two provided about the value of a teeny, tiny miniature horse. When they behave dramatically badly, they are less likely to kill you than the full-size version.

Unfortunately, while the Battle of the Stars was taking place, I found myself in a bit of a sticky wicket. The $700 Pony did not take kindly to the flurry of activity occurring at her right flank, not to mention that I think she had real concerns that BW might try to take her on next, so she required my undivided attention for quite some time, all of which involved a plethora of things tossed hither and thither, much laying on of the hands to calm the frantic pony and a general flurry of activity that did not take into account the volumes of boot polish I had splashed about while cleaning my boots.

Eventually calm was restored to our neck of the trailer parking, and around that time, The Instigator trotted past with her brood in tow. "Hoo, boy!" she called out in passing, "Pony looks good, but what happened to you?"

I looked down at my covered-with-boot-polish hands and realized, to my horror, that it was not just my hands covered with boot polish. "Oh, no," I whispered half to myself, half to the Pony. My boots looked great: they were black and shiny and returned almost to their original glow. I, however, was anything but glowing, There was boot polish everywhere—on my white shirt, on my tan breeches and, as I glanced in the side-view mirrors of my truck, all over my face.

Sighing a deep hopeless sigh and realizing that all of my planning to stay clean and be presentable was once again completely for naught, I grabbed my show jacket thinking that at least I would be able to cover up the boot polish stains on my shirt with a jacket.

Nope. No chance. My show jacket was still at home. Maybe even in a dry cleaning bag somewhere. The jacket I was holding in my hand was a black suit jacket. And don't think for one second that it had the slightest chance of masquerading as a show jacket. The cut of the jacket was late 1980s. It was something I hung onto for the sole purpose of wearing to funerals and nowhere else. Why it had been in the dry cleaning bag, I could not venture to guess, but it would certainly be better for me to appear without a jacket than with this, this imposter—this sad, not-even-close-to-an-imitation-of-a-riding-show jacket.

And, I left my belt at home. My two new spiffy $5 Warmit belts that would at least tidy this miserable mess up a little. At home.

But I am nothing if not optimistic, and it was time to make the best of it! I was not there to win any prizes, we have already ascertained, so what if I was not quite as spiffy as I would have liked to be. I hopped on the Pony and headed down to warm up.

In a hunter-type show, you have the opportunity to go into the ring you will be competing in and jump over the fences that you will be competing over. This is called schooling. In the eventing world, we would call this cheating. In eventing you don't get to jump over the jumps you would be jumping over while competing. You jump over jumps that are set far away from the jumps you will be competing over. This is called "warming up." Totally different.

I, being almost a professional horse trainer, made the executive decision that I would not "school" the fences in the ring like a hunter, but that I would "warm up" over some fences that I would not be "not-competing" over. This, of course, was a terrible mistake. The Pony had never seen fences like the ones she would be jumping over in the ring and any moron with half a brain would have realized that. In fact, most people probably would have realized that this whole stupid idea was a stupid idea, packed it up and gone home, but apparently I have been blessed with less than half a brain and went blithely on.

So, I headed down to the show rings, not to school, as we have already determined, but to warm up. Because this local horse park hosts many horse events, it just so happens that they have a cross-country course, and they had conveniently left up the cross-country warm-up fences. It was a comforting bit of home. I had been feeling a little bit lost and foreign, not to mention blackened and slightly sticky, among this crowd. Even at a local schooling show, the hunter folk just looked, well, so put together. There were spiffy Tailored Sportsman jackets, nifty puke-green Tailored Sportsman breeches and lovely contrasting show shirts. And I just looked tan and white and black all over.

But the show must go on, and I set to warming the Pony up. She was pretty rough around the edges, but we did the same sort of warm up that I would do for an eventual stadium round. Jump a fence. Stop. Turn around. Jump another fence. Stop. Turn around. Jump another fence. And so on. The Pony was doing OK. She has always displayed a little more enthusiasm than I would like upon landing, but she was performing up to expectation. The occasional bolt for the cross-country course not withstanding, I was pretty sure we would do okay in our four-fence and six-fence classes. Mostly pretty sure. Well, maybe I just wasn't thinking about it much.

The nicest thing about my warm up was that I was alone. The real hunter people were all schooling together in the show ring jumping over the jumps that they would be competing over. It was a little scary to watch. Kind of like an old-time demolition derby. Not that they were intentionally running into each other, but the fences were tiny, the riders and horses were pretty green and there were more than a few close calls. Unlike in eventing where we have prescribed rules for warming up that must be obeyed or you will be eliminated,[10] these folks jump fences any which way but loose with no regard for life or limb.

The announcer came on and announced that it was time to begin the show day. So the $700 Pony and I stopped warming up and sauntered over to the ring where we would be "not-competing." From an anthropological point of view, this is one of the more interesting points of the hunter scene. See, in the sports of dressage and eventing, you enter shows weeks before the actual day and are assigned a ride time several days before the show, so you know exactly when you are supposed to show up, warm up and then actually ride your prescribed test, etc. It's a pretty useful, easy way to go about things—and not at all the way hunter people do it.

Hunter people, quite the contrary, seem to go out of their way to insure that you not have the slightest possible idea when you might ride. In fact, they remind me a lot of the cable guy. You know, the guy who says he'll be by to install your cable between 8 am and 2 pm? And if you ask him why he can't tell you within a slightly closer time, he just laughs at you and asks you if you really *want* cable.

---

[10] This is one of the really cool things about eventing. The sport itself is so inherently dangerous that the people who make the rules do everything they can to mitigate the danger. For example, in any jumping warm up, the warm-up fences are flagged with a red flag on the right side and a white flag on the left side, and you are only allowed to jump with the red flag on your right hand side. If you jump it the wrong way, you get eliminated! Makes for a much safer warm up than the willy-nilly jumping that hunter people do in their schooling sessions—in my opinion, anyway.

Then he doesn't even bother to show up or even call to tell you that he can't make it that day. That's what a hunter show is like.

So, basically, you get there an hour or so before the show starts and you just hang out until they call your class. Luckily for me, the two-foot division was the first of the day. Pretty typically, they start with the fences as small as they go and then increase the size as the day progresses. So perhaps years from now the Pony will be ready for the 3-foot division and will go after lunch. But for right now, her division was ready to go just before breakfast.

The even funnier thing is that as soon as Announcer Man announced that the show was beginning, I stopped warming up and came on over expecting things to get rolling. This is not how it works at a hunter show! No indeed! In fact, when the Announcer Man announced it was time to clear the ring, even more people piled in to jump a few more jumps! Seriously! For those of us used to the rather stringent rules in the world of eventing and dressage where elimination lurks around every corner, this type of behavior is just shocking!

But it is how the hunter world works. So Announcer Man announced a few more times the show was ready to begin, and more people piled in to jump a few more jumps. Announcer Man made a few threatening comments to the effect that people really needed to clear the ring so that they could get started, and a few more people piled in. And when they were all done to their very own satisfaction, they sauntered out of the ring. And eventually, the ring was cleared and it was time to start.

There were only a handful of us in the two-foot division, and we lined up together by the in-gate, patiently awaiting the start of the class and the call for us to go in and jump our four fences.

I sat there atop the $700 Pony feeling vaguely discomforted. No matter how you sliced it, we were out of place. First, an adult riding a pony, while not all that unusual in dressage and eventing is just not done in the hunter world. The other riders in my division all had their lovely show jackets on and looked so tidy and nice. I didn't.

And all of the other horses in my division were braided. These were people who were serious about the two-foot division!

There we all sat, me in my odd attire, looking for all the world as though I had gotten lost on my way to a dressage show. And there sat my competition, all five of them, and call me paranoid but they were eyeing me.

At first I thought it was the clothes. I really did think it was possible they were staring at my clothes—or lack thereof, as I was the only rider anywhere in the vicinity of the horse park not wearing a jacket. Or maybe they were staring at my pony. I mean, as I mentioned, ponies are just not done, unless, of course, you happen to be under the age of 14, which I had not been for many a moon.

But they *were* staring at me! I was sure of it! Those hunter princesses in their Tailored Sportsman's were *staring* at me. Until, without warning, the hunter princess on the left, the one on the bright bay gelding, groomed within an inch of his life, his striking black mane beautifully braided, dropped her reins and clapped. Not applauded, as in applauded a good round in the ring, but glanced over at me, dropped her reins and clapped twice, like this: CLAP, CLAP.

She glared at me while she did it. A few moments passed.

And then the hunter princess on the bright bay gelding did it again: CLAP, CLAP. But this time she did it in tandem with the young lady on the dappled gray sitting next to her! They did it at the same time, in unison: CLAP, CLAP.

They glanced at each other, they glanced at the young lady sitting on the chestnut gelding to their left and they all glared in unison at me. And then *all three* of them did it again: CLAP, CLAP.

There were only two more people waiting to go into the class. And they were as engrossed in these goings on as I was. And it took them only a beat or two to *join in*! I have to admit I was beyond baffled at this point. All five of them glaring at me, and then glancing at each other and in unison, clapping their hands: CLAP, CLAP.

Apparently, the last two hunter princesses joining in the fun dispelled whatever was causing the glaring, because, by the time all five

of them were doing it, the first hunter princess was giggling so hard I thought she was going to fall off her horse. And it didn't take long before all five of them were giggling and snorting and generally carrying on as though there were a Seinfeld rerun going on in their heads. The joy did not spread to me, of course, because I had absolutely no idea why these morons were behaving so bizarrely, other than a sneaking suspicion that it had something to do with me.

At which point, the ring steward called the first rider in the ring. The hunter princess on the bright bay, wiped the tears of laughter from her eyes, took one last choking look at me and entered the ring. The rest of the hunter princess group discreetly moved away from me, giggling,

Wondering what in the heck could possibly be going on, I watched hunter princess #1 enter the ring. The ring steward apparently either took pity on me or decided that I was village idiot material and he could give me a hand relocating to a new village.

He tapped me on the knee, looked up at me (which is not very far to look up, remember, I am the only adult with a hundred miles mounted on a pony) and said earnestly, "Um, did you know you were, um, humming?"

I hacked it out like a hairball. "*Humming?* What to you mean *humming??!!*"

The steward looked left and right and leaned in really close, "Um, yeah, I don't want to embarrass you or anything but you have been sitting here for the past 10 minutes humming "If You're Happy and You Know It, Clap Your Hands." He looked me earnestly in the eye, "Over and over."

Unless you have ever had one of those "naked at work dreams" that turned out to be true (that is, you really *were* naked at work), you cannot begin to imagine the humiliation I felt at that moment. Heaven help me, an earworm had sprung to life, and my children were not there to save me! Strike that! Thank goodness my children were not there to witness my abject humiliation as a horde of hunter princesses made fun of me, to my face, while I stalwartly hummed on in complete oblivion!

My face morphed into a brilliant shade of crimson and stayed that way for the next day or so. And yet, worse humiliation was to come!

I rode the Pony into the ring for her round. It was a moment of naked, earnest truth. A moment when I realized I really should have "schooled" the fences in the ring instead of "warming up" by the cross-country course. A moment when I realized a split second too late that I had stopped to salute the judges, something you do in Eventing Land, but not in the hunter world. A moment when I approached the first fence that I realized that I had never actually jumped the Pony over a course of fences. The fact that there were a mere four fences probably saved my life, but I had never asked her to jump more than one fence and then stop. To ask her to suddenly jump a course of four fences in a row, especially after listening to an unrelenting chorus of "If You're Happy and You Know It" seemed to border on cruel and unusual punishment.

As I sputtered around the short course in fits and starts, the showing epiphanies were flowing like wine at a wedding! I suddenly remembered fistfuls of the stuff I had forgotten—stuff I really,

really should have practiced long before I got back in the ring, even in this pseudo-competition mode, like *how to ride a line*. I mean, really, I was like a little kid in the first grade showing up for calculus class, a happy smile on my face, "Oh, how hard can this really be? Come on, I can count to 10, watch me!"

Although I suppose that likening two-foot fences to calculus is a bit of a stretch. The $700 Pony could, and did, step over the itty bitty fences. So we got through it. It was only four fences. And they were only two feet off the ground. Even in slow motion it doesn't take that long to get around four fences. And I did not stand anywhere near the still giggling hunter princesses before the second class. I was afraid the heat from my face would cause them to break out in a sweat. No, really, I was just too embarrassed to be anywhere near them. I was afraid they would start clapping again.

We also survived our second class—all six of the two-foot fences. But not very well, and I have to say that I left the ring just a little discouraged and kicking myself for even going back to bother with the second class. I really should have just scratched and headed home. I sought counsel from The Instigator. Sort of.

"Hey, it's all your fault I'm here and I had a crappy time!" I shouted at her. "The Pony isn't ready to be doing this stuff!" I had a sudden flash back to the trainer/therapist. I hadn't even told her I was showing—probably because deep in my heart I knew she would have told me it was a bad idea.

But The Instigator, being The Instigator, was soothing and contrite, "Oh, you are so right! What were we thinking that the Pony should be out jumping? But did you know they have a dressage show next week? Maybe you should think about doing that."

"Hmm," that stupid part of my brain that seems to drive my intelligence bus muttered, "A dressage show? Yeah, yeah! That's a great idea!" So I forgave The Instigator for dragging me to my humiliation and packed it up and went home.

CHAPTER 11

The $700 Pony Begins Rolling and Thus Gathers No Moss, Part II: The Dressage Show Prep

And so I began planning for our dressage debut. As outlined in exquisite detail above, I can at least get the clothes right for this gig. The interesting thing about the show series that The Instigator suggested I enter, though, is that it is a series of very low-key schooling shows. So low key, in fact, that jackets and formal attire were not required. A pair of tan breeches, white shirt (with no stocktie) and clean boots were all that are required, so I was already way ahead of the curve.

Since the ultimate goal is to get the Pony to an event, the hunter show humiliation was actually a very good learning experience for me. It reminded me of all of the things I had forgotten about showing. Or at least the ones associated with the stadium jumping phase of eventing, which was probably 30 percent of the way to remembering all of the stuff that I needed to remember. I was pretty sure that when I actually got to a dressage show and a cross-country school that there would be a whole passel of new stuff that I had forgotten that would bubble to the surface.

Now if you will recall, the generally accepted lowest level of dressage is Training Level. You have to be able to walk, trot, canter, halt and have basic steering in place in order to execute any of these very basic, elementary tests. As the Pony did not really canter much at all yet, this was going to be a problem. Hence, I planned to enter the tests designed for the dressage challenged: Intro Tests A and B.

As detailed in a previous chapter, if Training Level is like knowing your ABCs, Intro, well, I'm not sure there is an analogy for Intro. Intro Test A requires that you trot into the arena, slow to a walk, then halt, which seems pretty simple unless you haven't properly installed brakes on your pony. You salute the judge, which you always do in dressage and eventing but *never* in hunter shows and then walk off. You walk a bit, then trot a bit, trot a circle, walk a bit more, change direction, trot a bit, trot a circle, then halt, salute and you are done. Easy peasy.

But I had been alerted to my own personal deficiencies at the hunter show so I now knew that I could be all too easily lulled into a false sense of security and have the whole mess come crashing down on me. So this time I would be prepared!

I decided that I would do a dry run of the dressage show a week or so *before* the dressage show. As the horse park is merely half an hour trailer drive from my house and I am an annual member and can go and use the facility any time I please, I decided I would head out early one morning to practice my tests in the dressage rings. Pleased as punch at my ability to think through and solve this problem, I arranged with my dear husband to watch our two wee children, packed up the Pony at dawn one hot summer day and headed over to the park.

I printed out a copy of Intro Tests A and B and tucked them into my back pocket. While in the fine sport of dressage, you can have someone "read" a test to you while you ride it, the vast majority of people memorize them. The lower level ones in particular are pretty short, so on the whole it's not hard to commit them to your brain and ride them from memory. And I was planning to memorize the test prior to the actual show date—probably on the drive over if we can use past history as a barometer of the future. So I hadn't gotten around to memorizing them yet and tucked them into my back pocket to read when I arrived at the horse park with the Pony.

The sport of dressage, being a horse sport, has its own saddles, bridles and other accoutrements designed to line the pockets of those people who make a living making and selling saddles, bridles and other accoutrements. I have a lovely dressage saddle that I have had for years that frankly makes me feel as though I am a much better rider than I actually am. I mean, I have a dressage saddle, so I must be a dressage rider, right? This is a bit like handing over keys for a Lamborghini to a 17-year-old kid who just got his driver's license: "Hey, you can drive, right? Give it a whirl!"

But I persist in thinking I am better than I am. Dressage saddle in hand, I tacked up the Pony and hopped on, heading for the riding rings. Now, the Pony had never seen a dressage ring before. She was boarded at a hunter barn, and it's not like they keep dressage rings around there! No, sir! So I made my usual thoughtless, stupid plan. I warmed her up in the general warm-up ring and then brought her up to the dressage ring to do a dry run on the test.

Here is a drawing of what a dressage ring looks like. If you ride in these things all the time, please move along. Otherwise, check it out. Notice that it is sharply rectangular and that there are letters carefully placed at very precise and specific increments around the ring. Also please note that the letters themselves appear to have been selected at random by a drunken gnome. There is no rhyme or reason.

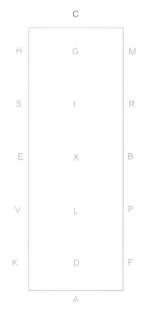

So, the basic premise of a dressage ring is that you are given a prescribed arena in which to execute your test. The letters indicate the places in the test where you execute transitions of some sort or another. You trot in and halt at X.[11] You walk and turn right at C. You trot at M. You execute a 20-meter circle at E, etc. Pretty simple, right?

The ring itself consists of an 18-inch fence set using highly technical tools to the specific measurement of a 20 by 60 meters (or 20 by 40 meters, for some tests).

I walked the $700 Pony into the ring in all its 18-inch-high glory. But there were no letters. That really was not all that surprising: the rings are left up all the time, but the people who run the shows only put the letters out for show days. Letters are expensive—you take care of them and keep them out of weather as much as you can. Besides, every moron who rides at even the most basic level of dressage knows where the letters belong in the ring and can ride approximately to where those letters are supposed to be.

Unless, maybe you are me, and you have not actually ridden in a dressage ring in a million years and suddenly realize that you have lost the key to that room in your brain where the placement of letters is stored. *Merde!* All this trouble to come up and ride my tests and I have absolutely no idea how the bloody test should go!

However, if you have had any experience with these things, you are probably wondering, hey, those Intro Tests you are doing are pretty easy! There are what, maybe eight movements? Surely you can figure out where you are going based on the directions the test gives you? Probably. But since I had not even looked at the tests until the very moment I rode up to the ring and noticed there were no letters, it would have been hard, at that exact moment, to say.

---

[11] I should point out that while X (along with G, I, L and D) is marked on the diagram, in real life it is a spot in the middle of the ring that is *not* actually marked with a letter. You are supposed to be able to guess where it is based on the location of the letters "E" and "B," which are placed on the outside of the ring. X is halfway between "E" and "B." Ditto for the other letters shown in the middle of the arena. Dressage, as I am sure you have ascertained, is a tricky sport.

I pulled the crumpled test sheet out of my breeches pocket for the purpose of checking out the test to see if I could figure out where I was supposed to be riding. Unfortunately, the Pony, clearly recognizing her place on the evolutionary ladder as "prey" found the rattling paper disturbing and took off in a dead run.

As I only had one hand on the reins and the other on the flapping test sheet, my ability to intervene was limited. The Pony was sadly in a traumatized panic and as she raced toward the edge of the dressage ring, I realized she was going to jump over it. Now, 18 inches is no big deal to jump over. Remember, I had shown her at two whole feet just the week prior, so it wasn't a height issue,

It was more an etiquette issue. You just don't jump over dressage fences. Ever. In part this is because the horse or pony is supposed to respect the ring as something to be ridden *inside of*, not *over*. It's hard to explain the nuance of this, but it is obvious if you are actually riding and competing—if your horse steps *over* the dressage ring, thereby leaving it at any time while competing, you are eliminated. Poof, end of story, pack it up and go home, girlfriend. There you are. One does not encourage leaping over, on or about dressage rings. In fact, I would go so far as to say that one actively *discourages* it.

But there was no stopping the Pony. It's not like I have installed great brakes on her to begin with and, besides, we had been working on jumping, so she was pretty well convinced this was what she was supposed to do. With a graceful leap, the Pony hopped over the dressage ring fence and bolted for wherever, with me flapping about up there, papers flying. In general it was a mess. It took a bit to finally slow her down and reorganize.

Reorganizing, my initial assessment was that things had gone south. First, the Pony was terrorized by the test paper, which I was required to read in order to even pretend that we were going to practice a dressage test.

Second, I had no idea how to actually ride the test given that I was not sure where the bloody letters were placed. I mean, some of it was easy, like right turn at C, but then the test did this funky diagonal thing that didn't make sense, although I think it would have made perfect sense if I had had a clue where the letters actually went. I mean, sure I could *guess* based on ancient knowledge dredged from the brain remnants the birth of my two children have left me, but the point of this adventure was to practice the actual test, not practice riding a test I *hoped* was the right one.

Third, and probably the most critical on the list, because 1 and 2 are really timing issues, I was feeling totally hosed as the Pony had used the dressage ring as a *hurdle!* Jiminy Cricket, this is just not done! And I feared a great foreshadowing of bad things to come.

I finally hopped off the quaking Pony long enough to commit the dressage tests to short term memory and resecure the test paper in my pocket. Then I hopped back on to try riding in the dressage ring again. As someone who seems to spend an inordinate amount of time solving the problems I create for myself, I am nothing if not always up for a challenge.

Reorganized, we reentered the ring, and I focused on keeping the Pony inside, which proved to be quite the difficult task. The Pony, you see, really does like to jump. She has discovered flight and is loathe to give it up, so her entire focus for the next half hour or so was jumping out of the ring. I could certainly understand where she was coming from. The way this dressage crap works, she was supposed to be trotting right up to this ring in exactly the same way we trot up to a fence we jump. Only instead of jumping it, we turn left or right. To the Pony, this must have been quite confusing. Why do you sometimes jump and other times you turn?

At some point years from now, when she is happily leaping over 3 ½-foot fences, we will look back at this and laugh: 18 inches for Pete's sake! But right now, 18 inches to 2 feet is her norm, so she is confused. In my utter and absolute lack of knowledge of training horses, I found myself using the hammer approach to solve this problem—trot right up to the fence and turn, turn, *turn*!

Not unexpectedly, this did not work well, particularly as it does not deviate much from how I jump her. She was getting quite excited—which is bad whether you are jumping or not—and she would get herself ready to leap. And I would turn her, she would get all sad and frustrated and this went on for half an hour or so before I accepted the reality that we were making no progress and headed home.

My poor dear husband and wee children were waiting with breakfast made for Mommy, and I was frankly not in a good mood. Not only had I failed to achieve my goal for the day, practicing two Simple-Simon tests that I was due to perform in public in a few days, but I realized that I had (a) made the situation worse than it would have been if I had not practiced at all, and (b) I now have an entirely different problem to solve.

So I went back again. This time, I had the foresight to determine the placement of the letters. One crisis out of the way, and in a flash of brilliance that I do believe is standard operating procedure for the usual dressage rider, I actually went ahead and memorized Intro Tests A and B prior to arriving at the horse park. This, of course, was designed to reduce the chance that the Pony would bolt off again if I tried to pull the test out of my pocket while I was riding her.

The only task for the day was to ride the tests. I decided this time to warm up in the dressage ring itself, thinking that I needed to acclimate the Pony to the show environment. I started by walking around the edge. The Pony thought she was going to get to jump and got excited. Not good. So I went back a step and just walked in a small circle in the middle of the ring. The Pony, still thinking we were going to jump, was still excited. This could be worse, I suppose, but it was certainly not getting any better.

We began trotting on our little circle. The Pony still thought we were going to jump. The Pony then noticed a small shadow on the ground, executed a perfect "10" Serengeti Slide and I met the dirt. Perhaps indicating that there is a higher likelihood that she will make an event horse than I have been giving her credit for, she raced over to the 18 inches of dressage ring and hopped over. Then she raced off into the sunrise, quite triumphant and happily free of me. *Merde!*

I eventually caught her, although my husband was late to work that day. And he was late to work the next two days, too, as I trailered her over every morning at dawn desperately trying to acclimate her to the dressage ring. The good news, I suppose, was that I really was getting my money's worth as a horse park member. And pecking away at the back of my brain was a reality that I keep trying to push back, which was that I was hauling over to the horse park on a daily basis to get ready to ride in a very small schooling show that is merely a tiny pebble stepping stone to the event I hope to eventually be able to do. Well, I suppose we all crawl before we walk, but it was feeling a bit like I was slithering along on my belly.

CHAPTER 12

A Stone Begins Rolling and Thus the Pony Gathers No Moss, Part 3: The Actual Dressage Show

The day of the dressage show dawned bright and cool, and I believed we were as ready as we could be at this point in the Pony's nontraining. By the last schooling session prior to the day of the dressage show, I had been keeping her in the ring about 90 percent of the time. While it did seem to me that she was not really "through" or "submissive" and all other stuff that she really should have been before she was really, really, ready to do a dressage test, I did believe I would be able to steer her in the prerequisite circles while staying inside the ring. Hey, you have to take your victories where you can get them.

Now dressage shows really are a gig I like. I mean, hunter shows are tough: you never know when you are going to ride, and all the riders warm up together like a huge flock of lemmings on horse-back, seemingly bent on self-annihilation. But dressage shows are much more my speed. You know exactly what time you are going to ride, warm up involves no jumping over immovable objects at high speeds and you ride your test all by yourself in a ring.

I really did feel that I could make a plan that made sense around a dressage show. I knew three days ahead of time that my ride time was 8:02 pm—half an hour past my youngest child's bedtime to be precise. But that knowledge gave me power. I called my beleaguered mother-in-law. Unlike my mother, who has to drive two hours to be beleaguered, my MIL is but 15 minutes away. I have to say that it makes it rather easy for me to take advantage of her kindness—which I do as often as I think I can get away with it.

In this case, I requested a drop-off time that left me with adequate time to take a deep breath upon dropping my children, return home, get the Pony appropriately and fetchingly ready for the dressage show, leave with plenty of time to get there, tack up and then warm up with undue stress—all for two tests that would take, in sum total, about 10 minutes to ride.

I dropped my two wee children off at 2 pm, which, if my brain cells can come together for just a moment, left me exactly six hours and two minutes to prepare for my ten minutes of glory.

Now the prep plan went as follows: bathe the Pony, braid the Pony, clean tack, shower, load tack and show clothes onto trailer load up and arrive at horse park around 6:30. Mount at 7:00, warm up for an hour, offer a quick prayer to the dressage gods, whoever they may be, that she stays in the ring, ride Test A, ride Test B and leave for home just about when the sun was setting.

Now braiding was touched on earlier as something the hunter princesses do and I did not do for the hunter show. Braiding is the fine art of, well, braiding your horse's mane into tiny little cornrows. It is a lovely, rather formal look when done well, and tragically flawed when not. There are two kinds of people in the world: those who love to braid and those who do not. As it turns out, I am in the former category (and for all of you thinking "former/latter/former/latter, which is which?" I'll help—I love to braid!).

I really do love it. I am fast and good so my braids always look lovely and don't take much time. I strongly suspect that people who don't like to braid are slow and probably not very good braiders. So, despite the fact that I would not braid her for the hunter show (which had more to do with the fact that my mindset was more about not-competing than not wanting to braid), I really did want to braid her for the dressage show. While it was quite possible I would be the only person at this local, low-key schooling show to have a braided horse, I was not deterred. I love to braid, wanted to braid and was planning to make darn sure there was enough time in my schedule to braid.

It was a good plan, particularly given that I had six hours and two minutes to execute. However, anyone who, at this point, thinks for one second that this plan is going to work should probably put this book down and step away. As a side note, I do wonder how I can continue to make and execute incredibly flawed plans without ever realizing ahead of time that my planning is so flawed. Ah, life is a learning exercise.

I arrived at my mother-in-law's at 2 pm. First mistake. Counting six hours and 2 minutes did not include thinking about dropping off, giving minute direction in the care and handling of my wee children (who see mother-in-law on a frequent enough basis that it's really like preaching to the choir) and then the requisite schmooze time. I mean, it's not like you can just drop them and run, right? They're *children*, not dry cleaning.

Of course, it does take *time,* actual ticking minutes, to drive from MIL's house back to our farm—probably 15 minutes on a good day. And it's not like I actually headed straight home. My brain was in six-hours-and-two-minutes-mode, also known as all-the-time-in-the-world-mode—a very, very dangerous state of mind for me.

What with the incredible freeing feeling of my two wee children safely in someone else's hands, I decided to make a few stops along the way. First, I stopped at Warmit without my two wee children. This is unmitigated joy in my book. I was clever enough to have a very specific list of things I required from Warmit; however, the sheer giddiness of being in this giant place of unadulterated commerce led me to browse a bit. And so the clock ticked.

I finally came down from my Warmit high and headed out to the car, still in all-the-time-in-the-world mode; I stopped at the local Wa-Wa for dinner. Now, those of you who know what a Wa-Wa is are saying, "Yuck! What could you possibly get for dinner at *Wa-Wa?*" Those of you who cannot imagine that a store of any repute would bestow upon themselves the moniker "Wa-Wa" do not live in New Jersey.

A Wa-Wa, I suppose, is the New Jersey equivalent to that old Southern staple, Piggly Wiggly. Everybody knows and loves The Pig! Well, all of us here in New Jersey love the Wild Geese. Not literally, of course, because nobody *really* loves real wild geese, but we all love Wa-Wa. Which is a convenience store that is named for the local Native American word meaning "wild geese." Just like the wild geese call: "*waaa-waaa.*" So there you have it. I stopped at Wa-Wa for a hot dog and a very large cup of coffee because I am a caffeine addict, and an afternoon without coffee is like an afternoon asleep on the couch, which is a bad thing. Thus, dinner at Wa-Wa.

Armed with caffeine, I stopped off to chat with one of my fellow farmers. In my world, there are two kinds of farmers: those who have not uttered a word since 1947 and those for whom quiet must equate to death, because you have never seen them without their mouths flapping. At least, that's my perspective. My husband has a slightly different point of view. While he agrees that there are two kinds of farmers, he would divide them into talkers and those who won't talk to women. But it's hard for me to gauge the validity of that one.

I would be one of the latter (*talker!*), as you can well imagine, so when I get together with another of my ilk, time can flow as fast and furiously as water over the great Niagara Falls. And what with all the time in the world on my hands, I stopped in to chat with Ron. We talked about the weather, the upcoming hay season and the impact the weather was having on the upcoming hay season, and then his cows and the impact my hay would have on his cows. And then about the freezer he would need to acquire in order to freeze the meat the cow would bring assuming I got reasonable hay despite the irascible weather, which somehow led to a short discussion on the history of Stalinist Russia. Good guy, that Ron. Didn't seem like much time was passing while we were jawing, but alas for that perception-versus-reality thing.

While Ron and I were debating how the fate of Russia, nay the world, would have been dramatically different had Stalin met an early demise, the "1812 Overture" rang out. **BOOM!** It was my husband. As usual. Before I met and married my wonderful husband, I was an occasional cell phone user. It was more for checking voicemail and the occasional emergency. Now it has become my primary means of communication, although mostly I just communicate with him.

Which is really an issue, because, as you may be able to guess without too many hints from me, I keep losing the blessed thing. I swear the man calls me once a day just to make sure that the incredibly expensive cell phone he purchased for me under the mistaken assumption that if it were really expensive I might take better care of it (ha!) is still in my possession. But that aside, the "1812 Overture" rang out, I answered it and dear husband told me he was on his way to his mom's to pick up our children. Pick up our children? Why? Because the work day was over and it was time for him to leave the office and head for home. Work day over? What in the heck time was it if the work day was over?

It was 5:30, which meant the Pony and I needed to leave for the show in exactly half an hour. And two minutes. Bidding the quickest goodbye in the history of farmer goodbyes to Ron, promising I would stop back in the next couple of days to take up the Stalin discussion again, I flew back to the farm.

I had exactly enough time to do one of the following: (a) bathe the Pony, (b) braid the Pony, (c) clean tack, or (d) shower. I had been hanging out with chickens and cow farmers, so my physical presence would have been considered offensive in closed quarters, but luckily I wouldn't be in closed quarters.

As a horseperson, I chose the thing that would be the most striking if I *didn't* do it, which was bathe the Pony. Hey, if she was shiny, glowing clean, my level of cleanliness—or lack thereof—would not be quite as evident. As for braiding, well, as much as I would have liked to, it sure as shooting isn't mandatory. And as for clean tack, well I could always run one of those gifts from heaven, a Murphy's® Oil Soap Wipe, over it.

Quick pause for commercial break here: if you don't have Murphy's Oil Soap Wipes in your home, car and tack trunk, run out right now and buy them! Right behind baby wipes, these little beauties are life savers! I don't use them all the time because they are pretty pricey, but if you have guests coming and no time, they do a great job making your wood furniture look all spiffy! And for tack? Well, what could be easier! Grab a wipe, wipe it down and then toss!

But back to our story. The frenzy began and the poor Pony did the best she could to stay calm in the advancing storm. She got the quickest scrub up of her short life, a goodly shot of Show Sheen for added glow and a quickie conditioner in her tail so I could fluff it out all nice and pretty. Tomorrow, of course, it would be full of the gunk the conditioner attracted like the gunk magnet conditioner truly is, but I was living for the moment.

I broke all previous land speed records in hustling the Pony onto the trailer and we were show-ward bound before she could blink. I had the tests propped up in front of me on the steering wheel for a last minute quick review. I couldn't really imagine anything more embarrassing than forgetting an Intro Level test, unless of course it was running into the back of someone while I was driving and rereading the tests.

As I reviewed the dressage tests, something suddenly occurred to me—something like one of those dawning realizations that kept popping up in front of me when I was trying so vainly to ride a hunter course with the Pony the prior week. It was one of those "you never go to a dressage show without" moments. A *watch*! Since you ride your test at a specific time (i.e., 8:02 pm), it makes good common sense to wear a timepiece that would allow you to keep track of time.

For most people, this would be a no-brainer. You wear a watch, right? Well, I don't. I'm one of those Luddite types who find them, I don't know, confining? I wore one in my youth, but the day I last took one off and swore I would never wear one again (which may have had something to do with the fact that I had hopped in the shower with it on and it was going to require the intervention of a "watch professional" to ever tick again), I felt so, I don't know, "liberated" I guess would be the right word. I haven't worn one in more than a decade.

Harking back to the years I competed prior to my two wee children, I could not recollect how I managed without one. There was some dim memory of maybe borrowing one for show days or maybe bringing a small battery-powered alarm clock? And technically, people who *really* event and do it well always wear a watch! That would be to check your time on cross-country. I just never got around to bothering with that. The horses I rode were generally slow enough that I wasn't going too fast to garner speed penalties and fast enough that if I didn't encounter any other penalty-enhancing behavior on the part of the equine, we would not be going slow enough to incur slow time faults.

But I am not a true Luddite, as I arrived at the show and was savvy enough to realize that my cell phone, otherwise the bane of my existence, would certainly serve as a fine stand-in for a watch. I jammed the little bugger in my pocket and started to tack up the Pony, figuring I would hand the cell phone to the ring steward before I actually entered the ring.

So I slapped my fine, almost-makes-me-look-like-a-professional-dressage-rider, dressage saddle on the Pony and headed toward the warmup.

The *really* nice thing about being at a schooling-type show, despite the presence of some actual real dressage riders is that there were others of my own ilk. There were certainly professionals in every corner of the show grounds, but as we waltzed toward the warmup, I spied fun-loving amateurs, happy neophytes and the occasional frank newbie.

In fact, there was a young lady at this particular venue who probably was at her very first show. I say this not just because it looked as though she were riding a lovely old campaigner, nor just because she was wearing a rather eclectic assortment of attire that looked a bit as though something old, something new, something borrowed and something blue had been cobbled together for this occasion. Nor was it just the enormous, beyond thrilled, I-almost-can't-believe-I-am-doing-this grin on her face. No. What made me suspect that this was the first time she would be entering the show ring was her entourage. Summing up mental images of Genghis Khan and his compatriots, "horde" was another word that sprang to mind. Mom and Dad were both present, and beaming, demonstrating the gene pool from whence the gleaming young lady's face arose.

Grandparents on both sides were apparently present, granddad #1 wielding the video recorder, Granddad #2 a late model digital still camera. The grandmas were stoic in the heat, dirt and general muss of a horse show, but fussing quietly over the young lady's boots and general attire. The old campaigner horse had the slightly bored, been-there-done-that look about him, but he was kind and wise enough to perk up when either granddad was in the process of recording these historic moments.

And there were more. I can't even quite imagine who all in the group were. Maybe trainer? Neighbors? Teachers? Aunts and uncles? I don't know, but there must have been 15 people milling about in this happy smiling group, with the young lady front and center, modestly enjoying the glow.

The bad news about this troop is that while they were utterly charming and it did my heart good to see them, they were also in my way. The show grounds has a number of warmup and show rings with relatively wide passageways between them. But this bunch, with all of their charm and innocence and rather obvious lack of horse knowledge, took up a huge amount of territory.

The Pony had been struggling since our arrival to maintain her composure. Her experiences at the horse park had been somewhat less than thrilling to date. I mean, she had witnessed the Miniature Horse/Boisterous Woman brawl, been humiliated by a group of hunter princesses and had been tormented over this dressage ring vs. jumping nonsense for hours on end. When we pulled into the horse park, I swear the thumping from the back of the trailer was her tapping out in Morse code, "Oh, no, not again!"

So, the Pony was a little brain fried and not displaying her best manners when we ran up against the Mongolian horde. They were swarming like locusts around their young rider, bolstering her confidence and clearly providing loving support. I did so hate to interrupt their reverie, but they were totally oblivious to me, and I really did need to get by. "Heads up," I quietly offered, in their general direction. They didn't even look up.

The Pony was fussing quite a bit, and I was almost thinking that it might be a good idea to just give up and go the long way around, when a pair of riders appeared behind me, also looking to get through. Now the Pony is a mare and girl horses can be kind of fussy about their personal space. They are actually fairly prone to kicking other horses that appear behind then. The young ladies who appeared behind me did not appear to be all that well versed in the cantankerous ways of girl horses and were blithely chatting with each other.

The Pony caught wind of the fellows behind her and pinned back her ears. Sensing that this situation had the potential to escalate to a not-so-great end, I increased the urgency of my request to the milling group ahead: "Hello, hello! Excuse me, heads up, please!"

Some of you might be thinking that my language was a little prissy, but I have a 3-year-old human child and really talk like this. Besides, these people were clearly new to the sport and I did not wish to give them a bad impression. At this point, the Chatty Cathy's behind me had halted, forward momentum blocked by the physical presence of the Pony's pretty chestnut butt and spectacular blond tail.

"Hey!" yelled the one on the left, "We need to get through!"

Muttering to myself about the decline of manners in this country, I looked over my shoulder, smiled nicely and said, "Just a moment, and I am sure these," and I turned away from them back toward the milling group, "NICE PEOPLE WILL STEP ASIDE AND LET US THROUGH."

The Pony took leave of swishing her tail to begin elevating her front end just a touch—a small rear to emphasize the fact that she was not happy with the lack of forward momentum and the proximity of the two horses on her butt. That seemed to do it for the neophytes. Clearly frightened by the raging creature in front of them, they parted like the proverbial Red Sea, and the Pony took the initiative and leaped into the space they had created. She swooshed her elegant tail in their faces as she rudely barged through, displaying terrible pony manners as I tried not to plow anyone over.

"Wow," I heard one of them mutter as we pushed past, "There goes a REAL dressage horse!"

Whew—dodged a bullet there! They didn't know enough to tell tragically bad behavior from dressage! I managed to sit a little taller and gave a little princess wave as I muscled my way through and even mustered up enough coordination to give the young lady a thumbs up! If possible, she smiled just a touch wider and waved her own little princess wave back. Ah, the joys of showing!

So the Pony was in a small whirling dervish frenzy by the time I actually got her into the warmup. Dressage being about harmony, lightness and obedience, the Pony was discordant, heavy and insubordinate. It was frustrating, because over the past few reschooling sessions as I tried to fix the problems I had caused, she finally *had* gotten a bit quieter about the dressage rings. But my job now was not to be frustrated by what could have been, but to make lemonade as best I could with what I had.

The warmup rings were a little intimidating as there were actual real dressage-type riders warming up to ride real dressage-type tests—not just fakers with nice dressage saddles. They were doing all kinds of cool stuff that the Pony and I cannot do, and I do not just mean cantering! But I sneaked off into a corner of a smaller ring where there was only one other rider and started to warm up, which in my case included walking, trotting and reminding the Pony that stopping once in a while is not only a good idea but is a mandatory part of the process.

The Pony was not steering all that well, nor really stopping. She was basically trotting around in her giraffe-on-crack mode and generally acting like a miniature runaway train. I did my best to stay as far away from the other rider as possible so as to minimize spreading the Pony's anxiety, horses being herd animals and all. Also, I was embarrassed and was trying to hide. Not an easy thing when you are riding an 800-pound animal, but I certainly did the best I could.

The other rider in the warm up actually looked to be a professional and even had her own entourage of lower-level-helper-type people. They were positioned on the outside of the ring, standing at attention. She would periodically bark something at them, by the looks of it, just to see how high they would jump. She was certainly not a happy, smiley-type person, but she seemed like a pretty competent rider, which she needed to be. While my Pony was behaving badly, her rather significantly larger horse was behaving much worse. I just tried to keep to myself as best I could.

The ring was more than large enough for the two of us, and as neither of us was having an easy time of it, you would think it would have been in both of our best interests to stay out of each other's way. But the other rider did seem to need a lot of space, and as much as I was trying to stay out of her way, she seemed determined to get in mine. So our paths were crossing.

Now I am the first to admit that I am not the world's most competent rider, but I was doing the best I could that particular day, and in my opinion, it is just not nice to pick on people having trouble. At one point, as I was walking, trying to refocus the hell-bent-on-self-destruction Pony, the other rider took the opportunity to give me a rather obvious, sour-faced once over.

She studiously looked away from me toward her entourage, glanced back at me to make sure I was listening, and pronounced in a very loud voice, "YOU KNOW, THERE ARE ONLY TWO

HARD THINGS ABOUT RIDING A HOT HORSE." She glanced over at me, just to double check that I had my listening ears on. "ONE IS THAT YOU MUST MOVE THEM FORWARD OFF YOUR LEG AT ALL TIMES AND TWO IS TO LET GO OF THEIR FACES."

She smirked at her support team, glanced over at me and in an apparent effort to give me a free lesson in how to solve my immediate problems, gave her horse a good nudge forward with her leg while giving with her hands.

Technically, of course, she was most correct. It is hard to do those things, particularly when your horse feels like she is careening out of control to start with. And it made me blush, since the comments were obviously directed at my incredibly ineffective handling of my Pony.

However, in her case, her horse took offense at the sudden pressure of her leg, took a huge lunging leap forward and bucked her off.

I almost fell off the Pony, too, mostly because I was laughing so hard. I trotted up to ask her if she was OK. Hitting the dirt had done nothing to improve her sour disposition, but she stood up, apparently in one piece, dusting herself off.

"Funny," I said, addressing her directly and happily making an enemy for life, "I think the hardest thing about riding horses is the ground!"

Snickering at my own temerity, I took the Pony off to another warmup ring to prepare for our ultimate entrance to the dressage ring.

The Pony actually did settle a bit and as we trotted around, practicing the moronically simple up-and-down transitions of Intro Test A. Then the next hurdle arose—the entrance whistle. This would be one of the many things about showing that I had forgotten about entirely, but that immediate proximity to the actual show rings brought to the surface.

If you are shaking your head wondering what the heck I am talking about, let me provide some background. The way a dressage test works is that you get a few moments to ride around the outside of the dressage ring to acquaint your beast with the locale, give your number to the scribe and generally prepare for the actual moment of first judging. At some point, the judge blows a whistle or rings a bell and you then have 45 seconds to get your butt in the ring or be disqualified.

I haven't seen many horses for whom this is an issue, but my last mare was one of them. She got over it in time, of course, but for the first year that I showed her, she would warm up beautifully, trot around the outside of the dressage ring quietly, submissively, lovely—until the moment she heard bell or whistle. At that moment, her eyes would bug out and she would leap forward and bolt.

Now you're not being judged on your time outside the ring. Period. End of story. While riding around the outside of the ring prior to your test, you can fall off and break your left knee cap, but as long as you are in the ring within 45 seconds after that whistle blows and ride your test reasonably well, no matter that your kneecap is shattered, you can receive the elusive 60 percent-plus score.

But come on! Judges are human and they are judging horses on "submission" and "obedience!" If you horse displays all the aplomb of a crack addict, you might think they would end up a little bit prejudiced on the submission and obedience scores. Although my judge friends assure me not.

But in moving away from the larger warm-up ring to one right next to my eventual show ring, I moved into a place where we could hear the, in this case, enormous cow bell, and I could gauge with at least a few minutes to prepare, how the Pony would react to the long, loud chime of the cow bell. The good news is that she didn't bolt the first time she heard it. The bad news is that she froze. And I mean froze solid, craning her neck up as high as she could stretch it and freezing. Not exactly the picture of submission or obedience. Ah, well, I thought, I had 45 seconds to get her unfrozen and into the ring. As long as I warmed up near the entrance to the ring, I stood a good chance of making it.

And in fact, as our ride time of 8:02 neared and the final riders prior to us headed into the ring, she continued to freeze every time she heard the resounding cow bell. The wild-eyed look of terror was not calming my fears about her future performance at all, I have to say. I was beginning to sigh to myself, thinking, this was almost as bad an idea as the hunter show.

The good news, though, was that this local show ran with startling efficiency. (Have I mentioned that I *love* dressage shows?) The ring stewards gave me the run down of which horses were going ahead of me, so I didn't even need to keep track of the time, as I was able to just count down the horses ahead of me—four, then three, two and finally the last person ahead of me finished her test and we were up.

I trotted the softly snorting, suspicious Pony up to the judge's stand, gave them my number and trotted off, preparing for the moment that the bell would ring and she would freeze. It came as expected. The judge range the bell, the Pony froze on the spot and aided by a significant amount of begging and pleading on my part to move—so much for obedience and submission—off we went on our way to our debut at Intro Test A.

So, it's easy. You trot in, slow to a walk and then halt. You are supposed to halt at "X" although, as I pointed out earlier, "X" is a mythical letter in the middle of the arena. It is an easy place for the judge to imagine, because it is strategically placed parallel to letters on the edges of the ring. It's a little harder for the rider, as you are trying to look forward and steer—and even harder if the braking system on your pony was not properly installed to begin with.

But we stopped somewhere in the general vicinity of X. Close enough that I felt good about it, but not close enough for me to think that there was any chance that the Pony would break the baseline score of 60 percent. OK, it was a pretty bad halt.

Intro Test A is the easiest dressage test ever designed for a human to execute. After the halt and salute at X, you walk off toward the judge, make a right turn and then, finally, excruciating minutes after you have entered this white ring of hell, you finally get to trot.

The upward transition to trot happened to be on the Pony's "good" side (she would essentially be "right handed"), and I was looking forward to it being the highlight of the test—the glowing moment that would cancel out subsequent and sadly, greater in quantity, bad moments. However, at that particular moment, the moment of the upward transition, the decision to stuff my cell phone in my breeches pocket and then forget that it was there proved to be not good thinking on my part.

Coinciding with the moment that I asked the Pony for the necessary upward transition, my cell phone rang. If I had thought to put it on vibrate, or possibly, even a reasonably quiet ring, I could probably have pulled the situation off with some degree of aplomb. However, there was just no way to maintain composure in the face of the "1812 Overture" (with cannon) at double maximum volume. **BOOM!**

The Pony, in the process of acknowledging and executing the trot transition, froze in place, quiet and still as a statue, one hind foot slightly elevated. As did I. I mean, what exactly was I going to do?

The first cycle of the "1812 Overture" rang on—***BOOM!*** And the second began— ***BOOM***! The Pony unfroze long enough to turn her frightened eyes toward me, begging me not to reprise "If You're Happy and You Know It." Thinking fast, I dropped my left rein and began swatting at the phone in my breeches pocket, thinking that if a million monkeys typing for a million years could come up with *Romeo and Juliet,* surely I could manage to hit the mute button.

What I hit instead was the button for my speaker phone. Good news, phone stopped ringing. Bad news, husband came on. Double, megawatt volume. "Hello," he said "Hello? HELLO? Hey, it's me, are you there?" I was trying to kick the Pony forward at this point. I mean, she was supposed to be trotting, not just standing there! I glanced over to the judge. She looked a bit stony faced and the scribe was giggling. That couldn't be good.

I started swatting at the cell phone again, thinking longingly about that mute button. Please, oh, please, I silently begged don't. But it was too late.

"Hey, are you there?" he shouted again. Discretion being the better part of valor, I gave up. I doubled over and hissed into my breeches pocket, "NOT NOW!" Swatted the phone into silence, picked up the dropped rein, applied leg and prepared to resume the test.

And just as the Pony, shuddering quietly, regained enough composure to resume the test, the judge rang the enormous chiming cow bell. Now the ringing of the bell signals two things: the beginning of the test, which is a good thing and was a hurdle we had already overcome because, of course, you are not technically being judged at that point (although I have already pointed out that with the kind of disobedience I am used to from horses at bell ringing, unless the test was magically free flowing and has somehow erased all memory of the bell ringing faux pas, it has got to have remained etched on the judges' brain at the point that they are thinking about the elusive submission and obedience scores).

And I have quite lost the point I was trying to make. Where was I?

Oh, so the *second* time the bell is rung is for going off course, which in layman's terms means that you have made a mistake. If you have somehow bone-headedly done this, which shockingly enough has happened to me at least once and probably more like at least 47 times, even in my limited dressage experience, you get a major deduction from your score. It is a big mistake to make a mistake of course!

And in this case, it was one of those weird technical things. I mean, I didn't really go "off course." It's not like I went left instead of right or executed a left-lead canter instead of a right-lead canter. I was just standing stock still for an extended period of time swatting weirdly at myself and whispering into my breeches pocket instead of quietly trotting off. I mean, given the length and difficulty of Intro Test A, I had probably been parked at that particular location in the ring longer than it took most people to actually ride the entire test. But all of that said, the bell was ringing, and it meant that I was having serious points deducted.

In fact, there were several reasons that the judge might have been ringing the bell. For example "use of voice" is strictly prohibited in the dressage ring, which means you may not speak to your horse, cluck, curse (even under your breath) or in any manner "use your voice" in the dressage ring. Bellows of pain if you fall on your butt are not even OK, since you are not eliminated for falling and can hop back up and continue bravely on. So it is very possible that the judge was sternly ringing the bell to notify me that she had heard me hissing at my husband and whether that was a secret code to notify the Pony of something or another or, even if it really was me just hissing at my husband, it was an illegal use of voice and I was being appropriately reprimanded.

A second possibility is that the judge was ringing the bell because I was standing still versus trotting. The movement called for was trotting, of course, and the Pony was not. This seemed the most logical to me, although frankly at the moment she rang the bell and the poor, already-terrified Pony, who was poised and in fact had come to life and had lifted her left front foot a millimeter toward forward momentum, refroze at the terrifying sound of the cow bell.

A third possibility is that at some point the United States Equestrian Federation had passed a rule not allowing cell phones in the dressage ring. Cell phones are clearly banned from eventing, so if I were at an event, I would have been eliminated, no questions asked. Although I did quickly scan the USEF rules when I got home and did not locate a ban on cell phones, it is very possible there is one and I missed it.

But regardless of the reason for the bell, the bell was rung. The clock was ticking and there we stood.

Now if I were to ask you what the similarities between dressage and baseball are, what would you say? Stupid light-colored outfits for people who can possibly end up in the dirt? True, but that's not what I meant. No, it's so easy! Three strikes and you're out! If you make one error of course, you get two penalty points, which really kills you because of how they are calculated into your final score. A second error gets you four points deducted which means you might as well hang up your dressage whip for this particular score. And a third error of course? Well, as they say in baseball, "You're *out*!"

So my greatest fear at that very second, the second that the judge rang the bell re-igniting the Pony's terror, which brought to mind the phrase "infinite loop," was that if I could not get her kick-started before the judge rang the bell for the *second* "error of course," I was doomed, doomed to get the *third* bell and be eliminated!

I suspect that in the history of "dressage for losers," also known as Intro, and specifically, Test A, a test that only has nine movements, that there has been no human being who has actually been eliminated for an "error of course." I mean, you basically have to get a third of the movements wrong in order to be eliminated.

Sure enough, as I was looking more and more frantic and starting to whomp the pony on her sensitive little sides with my heels, just as she was starting to come out of her terrified state, just as she lifted her little right front foot again to begin forward momentum, the judge range the bell for the second time.

The show I was attending is a friendly little show, and the judge was being rather friendly I am sure. I suspect that she gave me more time than she would at a larger show or in a more important test to resolve my issues, but by this point, I was causing the show to run late, and frankly, it was starting to get dark.

I will also point out that there is yet another very important rule that we have not yet considered. That would be the "20-second" rule. Specifically, Article 1922, section 7.12 of the USEF Rulebook, which states that if you sit around with your butt hanging out for 20 seconds, you get the proverbial hook. I have to say in hindsight the judge likely gave us more than the requisite 20 seconds to get our acts together. But as the Pony continued to stall, time and daylight and the judge's patience were running short!

Be that as it may, I really, really wanted to finish the test. So while I was kicking the Pony with great force, I also I sent pleading and slightly hysterical looks to the judge. Please, I silently begged, please, please don't ring that bell again! Just give her a minute to compose herself and let her go!

I could see the indecision on the judge's face in the slowly darkening light. I mean the judge is, by her very nature, an expert horseperson, right? So she knew what was happening. The Pony had been freaked out by the first ringing of the bell, then the phone, then the bell, then the bell again. I could see the judge sitting in her judge's box with her hand on the bell. Hesitating. She knew this was the most basic level a horse could possibly compete at, and she really did want to give me a chance.

There was a look of concern on the scribe's face, and they were whispering back and forth. I was using all of my pleading eye power, and just as I could see the judge beginning to shake her head in the negative, just as she was beginning to lift her hand to ring that bell for the third and final time, signaling a total and absolute failure of the Pony's first attempt at dressage, the Pony rose to the occasion and resumed forward motion.

The scribe burst into applause. I shot her a terrified glance just in case the sound of two hands clapping was more than the frazzled pony could handle. She quit instantly and got back to work while the Pony went on stalwartly.

The rest of the test was about as you might expect: anti-climactic. The Pony finished the remaining handful of movements in less time than it had taken to "reboot" herself, as it were, and I saluted with studied aplomb to finish the test.

This is the moment in a schooling show when a judge has the opportunity to offer some insight to the rider, to provide her with some guidance and help with her problems. Perhaps the judge gives the rider a tip or two that will help her improve her score the next time around.

There was silence from the judge's box.

The silence was extended. The judge was looking first at me, then at the Pony. Then at me again. Back and forth. Back and forth. Me. Pony. Me. Pony. Finally, she sighed. "Honey," she threw her hands up in the air, "I don't even know where to begin!"

Humiliated, I shrunk a little. I mean, surely she could come up with *something* to say! Something nice would be nice, of course, but helpful would be best. The judge could probably see my chin quivering even in the dimming light. Searching for something, she finally said, "Well," hesitating, as though even this morsel was more than she really cared to dish out to so pathetic a pair as the Pony and I me. She continued, again giving me and the Pony the once over, "She sure has a nice tail, doesn't she?"

CHAPTER 13

A Stone Begins Rolling and Thus the Pony Gathers No Moss, Part IV: A Second Dressage Show and Cross-Country School

The good news about our foray into the dressage world was that the second test went a little better than the first. Although, how could it have been worse? It was still frankly appalling, but significantly less horrendous than the first. And it turned out that the rest of the crowd there was also practicing fairly atrocious dressage, so the Pony went home with a blue ribbon *(first place?)* and a pretty yellow ribbon (*third, and, yes, there were more than three riders in the test!*). Which, shockingly, made me quite the star among my non-horseperson friends. My husband, for example, was thrilled to see me slouch in with these nifty ribbons.

"You won?" His incredulity was palpable, which was understandable. I mean, the man has seen me ride the Pony. And while he is not a knowledgeable horseperson, per se, he has a pretty good eye.

"Yeah," I sighed. "But it was tragic. No. Worse than tragic." I thought about it for a minute. "What's worse than tragic?"

"Catastrophic?" suggested Mr. Thesaurus. "Maybe 'wretched'?"

"Yeah," I sighed again. "Wretched would about describe it."

"But," he added, while, stroking the blue ribbon, "You won! We need to hang this thing up." He promptly hung it on a spot on the wall that every person walking into our home could not possibly miss unless they were legally blind.

My mom came over the next day. "You *won*!" she exclaimed. She hugged me. "How exciting! That cheap little pony of yours must be coming along."

"Well, Mom," I started gearing up for the shameful tale.

She cut me off, "Now, I know you are going to tell me some far-fetched story about how awful it was."

"Wretched, Mom, it was wretched!" I wailed.

Mothers have an important job in this world, and mine is pretty good at it. "It couldn't have been that wretched if you won! For heaven's sake," she hugged me again, "Congratulations on winning!"

Some friends came over on Sunday for dinner, and it was the same routine. There were a few ribbons hanging on the wall and everyone oohhhed and ahhhed over them. "Look, you *won*!" The ribbons *were* pretty, particularly the blue one. And they did look nice with the ribbons we had picked up at the hunter show (yes, there were only five and six people in our two classes, so we ended up fifth and sixth). I had to admit, I did like seeing them hanging on the wall.

But let's face it, winning in a dressage show is not what it is all about. Remember all that nonsense a few chapters ago about scores? Remember that breaking 60 percent is really important? If you can't do that, well, you probably shouldn't be out there.

I didn't break 60 percent, even in the class I won—and it's not like it was even close to 60 percent! We're talking mid 50s, and, frankly, it was well deserved! In truth, I thought the judge had been quite generous to give me a score in the mid 50s. So, it was back to the drawing board. I mean, if I couldn't do a *walk-trot* test that was worthy of a barely acceptable 60%, we weren't in very good shape, were we?

So I called my trainer/therapist. After the hunter show debacle I had at least alerted her to the fact that I was planning to attend a dressage show. Since we were doing a walk/trot test in a venue the Pony was familiar with, she thought it was a fine idea, so I called to let her know how it had gone.

"Wretched!" I wailed, and gave her the gory details.

She whistled. "Wow!" A few seconds of silence on the phone. She knew I wasn't exaggerating the dismal performance. "50 percent?" she asked.

"Mid 50s," I admitted.

"Ah," said the all-knowing trainer/therapist, "A generous judge feeling sorry for the newbie?"

I nodded miserably, maybe even ruefully, and agreed with her. You will notice that at no point did the trainer/therapist ask me where I placed in the class—because it did not matter!

"Alright," she said briskly, "You have to get your butt in gear. The next show is in two weeks? If you can get over here for a lesson a couple of times in the next two weeks, we'll see what we can do."

It was mid-summer by this point and last winter's dream of schooling the Pony, having a short, but successful competitive season and selling her for a boatload more than I paid for her was just not happening at the speed at which I expected. If you had told me when I bought her that eight months later she barely would be cantering, I would have laughed at you.

But here we were. Part of it was that the Pony had started out greener than green, complete with some built in bad habits that needed to be reset. Part of it was that I was not the most effective rider *prior* to taking three years off and now could probably be best described as "ineffective." And part of it was that frankly the Pony wasn't really the highest thing on my priority list. I rode pretty regularly, but life events intervened more than I cared to think and certainly more than I would have predicted, so her progress was slow.

But as the trainer/therapist pointed out, we had seen improvement. If I could spend a little more time with her and, consequently on the Golden Pathway, progress could be had! So I committed to finding appropriate childcare for my two wee children, and the Pony and I headed over to the trainer/therapist's for several stops on the Golden Pathway.

We were fairly focused on the upcoming dressage show, so the trainer/therapist and I did not have a chance to work on her jumping at all. Now, as clearly outlined in Chapter 9, jumping is pretty integral to eventing. And I had been working on that a bit as my foray to the hunter show attested. But if dressage was only going so-so, the jumping stuff was going really poorly, which actually makes perfect sense. Any moron can tell you that you don't jump a horse that isn't going well on the flat. But I think I had gotten a little caught up in my goals. I did persist in trying to jump, despite the fact that it wasn't going well. I just kept putting on my rose-colored glasses and thinking, "Well, it's going *better,*" even though it really wasn't.

But since we were focused on the dressage show, I didn't really share much of our jumping issues with the trainer/therapist. In fact, since I ended up with a ride time around 6 pm and a friend of mine from the trainer/therapist's barn was also going to show, the trainer/therapist decided she would come along and we could all do a cross-country school after the dressage show was over. It was a great opportunity for all—a real cross-country school—the final missing puzzle piece for an event! I was pretty excited and was able to conveniently block out all that stuff about how badly the Pony was actually jumping.

And so for our second dressage outing, we were much, much better prepared on many fronts.

My mother-in-law, pretty thrilled that I had actually won the first "race" while she was watching the wee ones, was happy enough to take them again for our next "race." My ride time was two hours earlier this time, but I couldn't justify dropping the children off any earlier than 2 pm. So I had to do the best I could with much less time to work with.

Having ostensibly learned from my previous dressage show attempt, I decided this time that I would clean tack and load the trailer the day before, leaving only bathing the Pony for the day of the show. I also remembered to count the drive time to and from my mother-in-law's in my time schedule. And as of kiddie drop-off time, everything was right on track. I dropped the children off, schmoozed for the necessary amount of time, hopped in my car for the 15–minute drive home, for which I had allotted 15 minutes, when my cell phone let loose its deafening cannon shot: *BOOM!*

I picked up the thing, which if you have been paying attention, is illegal in the state of New Jersey. I do always glance around to see if there is an officer of the law lurking nearby, but really, what I need to do is get my hands-free unit working. I glanced down at the plethora of cup-holders that act as repositories for dirt, grime, old bits of food and anything else that happens to fall to ground level in my car. Yep, the hands-free thing was gathering grime and old bits of fast food French fries in the bottom of one of my cup holders.

When my husband first bought me the fancy-schmancy new phone, I immediately tried to get the hands-free thingy to work. Unfortunately, the first step was befuddling and resulted in a call to the cell phone company, who proved to be absolutely no help at all, which, I believe, is in their job description and is the measure against which they receive raises and bonuses every year. If you really want to tick off a cell phone company person, tell him or her you are going to send a letter to the boss saying how *helpful* the person was. Send one of those and the cell phone guy will surely be fired!

Ultimately the guy I was talking to told me that I needed to let the phone and my hands-free sit for 24 hours and then try again. I mean, what a pitiful, stupid thing to say! Of course 24 hours isn't going to fix the problem! All it is going to do is get me off the phone with you, and you are going to watch your caller ID and when my phone number comes up in 24-and-a-half hours you will make darn sure one of your colleagues picks the phone up instead of you!

But I digress. The cell phone rang, and miscreant that I am, I answered it. Good thing, too, because it turned out that a 100 little lives hung on my answering that phone. It was my local baby chick store, reminding me that the 100 baby chicks I had ordered had been hatched the day before and when in the heck was I going to come get them?

And now I shall reveal my deepest, darkest secret. I do like chickens quite a lot. I have 150 or so layer hens who dutifully lay eggs, which I sell for a small profit. I also like chickens, with, um, barbeque sauce. OK, I'll come right out and say it: during the summer I raise meat chickens. Yes it's true. From May through September, I raise several hundred chickens whose only job is to eat in order to grow as big as they can, as quickly as they can, as naturally as they can, so I can sell them for as much money as I can get. Hey, it's a living.

Interestingly, most baby chicks are shipped via U.S. Mail. No kidding! Baby chicks are a fascinating dichotomy of incredible resilience and incredible fragility. They easily live 48 hours after pecking their way out of the shell without food and water. Getting them chilled at all, though, is a death sentence. So there is a cottage industry in this country of hatching baby chicks and shipping them all over.

In our case, though, the baby chick store is only half an hour from my house, so it just seems more humane to spend an hour picking them up rather than having them shipped to my post office. Although, since I do eat them after they spend nine weeks on my farm, my definition of "humane" might be considered suspect.

Luckily, when the call came, I was still on the road after dropping off my wee children, so gnawing my nails anxiously, I set a course for the baby chick store. Doing the calculations in my head, I was just going to make it—to the dressage show, that is. Remember the dressage show? I would not be able to bathe self— or Pony, but I would get to the horse park in time to warm up for the necessary hour to settle the Pony and then go for the scheduled cross-country school with the trainer/therapist. Hot dog!

Blasting to the baby chick store at the speed of light and hoping that I would not get a speeding ticket to ruin a nearly perfect day, I left the car running in the parking lot, raced in, grabbed the small box of peeping baby chicks and bolted.

It is a small box because when shipping baby chicks, they are squashed into a seemingly tiny space. That small space is pretty critical because baby chicks must be kept exceedingly warm in order to survive—a minimum of 95 degrees to be precise. So they are packed into tiny shipping boxes in order that they stay warm and cozy—and alive.

Because I had forgotten that the chicks were coming, I wasn't really ready for them, which means I had not set up a chick brooder. But since necessity is the mother—or at least great aunt of invention—I arrived home and quickly set to building a chick brooder out of available materials.

Now a "chick brooder" is nothing more than a space set aside to raise baby chicks. It needs to be draft free and warm, but as long as the sides are high enough to contain the chicks, it can be a cardboard box, a Rubbermaid container or any old lot of stuff that you prop up to contain them. In this case, reflecting some tragic irony, I used the transport crates that take my fully grown chickens to their ultimate end.

I put a heat lamp in the middle of the chicken crate chick brooder to ensure the temperature stayed in the chick-alive zone. Since it was early August and thus 105 degrees with 150 percent humidity outside, I wasn't really worried about keeping them warm.

The next issue was a waterer. I have a number of appropriate watering containers for tiny baby chicks, but they were all in use. I brood the chicks in batches and happened to have quite a few going at this point, so appropriate water containers were scarce.

As I have pointed out, baby chicks are inherently quite fragile. Ten percent brooder mortality is around the norm. They are so fragile it doesn't take much to send a baby chick to baby chick heaven. Squashing sadly happens, and certainly Psycho Mutt would turn herself inside out for one of these delectable fluffy hors d'oeuvres. But what will kill them quicker than anything is getting them wet. They are just not designed to take it; it chills them and they just turn up their little claws.

I am proud to say that I had zero percent brooder mortality for the first couple hundred chicks I brooded, which is really unheard of. Of course, I brooded those chicks in my living room. And if you have ever woken up in the middle of the night to the sound of 100 four-week-old chicks rampaging through your house (they staged a brooder break out), suddenly ten percent mortality looks pretty reasonable.

The lack of appropriate waterer was a bit troubling. A good chick waterer allows the chicks to dip their little beaks into hydrating water, but does not allow them to hop into it or otherwise submerse themselves. The baby chicks are very cute but not all that bright. Immersion leads to wet chicks, which leads to shivering chicks, which leads to chicks in a state we don't want to think about. If you must go there, imagine little tiny, fluffy adorable chicks with little cartoon x's over their eyes. Yeah, that's what I mean.

But with the clock ticking, I decided to take a gamble—a gamble that if I put out a simple tin of water in 105-degree heat and 150 percent humidity that the chicks would survive until I could return from my "Dressage Debut Part Two" and take more appropriate care of them.

The good news for the chicks is that it didn't take long for me to realize that I was not the Lotto Grand Prize Winner. Those downy little bits of fluff immediately immersed themselves in the inappropriate waterer and began shivering. All hundred of them. I yelled and waved to them, but it's not like I could just go tromping in there to keep them out of the inappropriate waterer. First, they were thirsty and needed to drink. Second, if I went tromping in there like some nightmare chick Godzilla, I would probably squash a few in my haste.

It was all good, though, because at least I knew I was on my way to a lot of dead chicks pretty quickly, which made it easy to do the right thing. I mean, if they had waited to start shivering until after I had left with the Pony, they probably would not have still been shivering when we made our triumphant return, if you know what I mean.

"OK, OK, little chicks," I murmured to their shivering little selves, wiping the dripping sweat from my brow. "Give me a minute and I will save your fluffy little lives." Tragically ironic in so many ways, of course. I mean, first I put them in mortal danger by giving them a clearly inappropriate water source. Then I chastise them for doing what comes naturally—drinking. Then I complain that I have to take the time to save their fluffy little lives. All so that I can "process" them in nine weeks and sell them for $3.99 a pound. Maybe "ironic" doesn't go far enough.

But there you have it. Farmer, responsibility to livestock is thine! I set about saving the chicks I had nearly snuffed. While it was time consuming, it was not difficult. These particular chicks, because they were newly hatched and had just eaten their first meal and had bathed in their first drink, would be fine for a few hours without food and water again if I could just repackage them in their original box and get a heat lamp on them. The combination of the squashing together and the heat lamp would provide enough heat to reconstitute them (unless, of course, I got the heat lamp too hot, in which case we would be having chick nuggets fricassee for dinner).

Crossing my fingers that I could get the heat lamp positioned just so, I went about capturing each and every one of the 100 bitty chicks, gently daubing them with a towel to remove as much excess moisture as I could and carefully repackaging them into their mailing container. Easier said than done, of course, because the little buggers, soaked and shivering as they were, were fast and nimble on their tiny claws. And I had given them way, way too much brooder space.

The danger in this whole exercise, of course, was the second leading cause of chick death: squishing. They little buggers are so fragile that stepping on them or otherwise smushing them also results in those sad little X's over baby chick eyes. And so it was with the greatest, tenderest care, all the while a little voice in the back of my head running an endless loop of Intro Test A and Intro Test B, that I rounded up the 100 baby chicks.

As this was literally a life-and-death situation, I kept the test voice at bay until the chicks were all reboxed and carefully positioned under the heat lamp. I put a thermometer down inside the box and waited and waited and waited until I was absolutely sure that that temperature had stabilized before I lifted my head and returned my thoughts to the Pony.

Time stands still for no man, and I can assure you that it had not made an exception for me while I was rescuing baby chicks. In fact, I could have sworn that it must have sped up. Surely it could not be 4:20 already! Good heavens, I wasn't even going to be able to brush out the Pony's famously luxurious tail, thereby securing the luxurious tail points that had probably won us a class the first time around!

But I quickly loaded up the Pony, flew to the horse park, warmed up and executed two fine walk/trot tests. Not perfect by a long shot, but who knew she had it in her? The Pony was pretty obedient, supple, etc. I even got a 6 for my rider score, while she got all 7s, which speaks volumes about the Pony vs. me, don't you think?

It was also possible that the very presence of the trainer/therapist on the show grounds propelled the Pony closer to the Golden Pathway than she and I could normally get on our own.

The scores she received on her tests were in the high 60s—the really high 60s! Personally, I thought they were inflated, as all of the scores for the day were a little on the high side, but I still felt good about the tests, which perhaps made me smile a little smugly as I picked up another blue ribbon (and another yellow one, if you happen to be keeping track).

The trainer/therapist was a little less sanguine about the whole experience. She thought the Pony did much better (considering my description of the previous outing), but she agreed that the judging had been generous, and while the test was not bad, it was a walk-trot test that consisted of nine movements, so it was nothing to write home to Mom about.

But I was pretty happy—progress! And now it was time for a cross-country school! Ah, running and jumping cross-country! This what eventing is all about! The torment of the hunter show and the machinations of Dressage Debut Parts One and Two were really all about getting to an event, and eventing is all about cross-country!

Off we dashed to prepare for our cross-country school! And prepare we must! As many fine eventing coaches, including but not limited to Lucinda Greene have oft been heard to say, "You wouldn't go into battle without your rifle, so why would you go cross-country unarmed!" Seriously.

So on went the special sticky palm gloves (originally designed for use in the NFL for catching footballs, believe it or not) for better grip on the reins in case of a torrential downpour. On went the special rubber reins to enhance the performance of the special sticky palm gloves should that skies open (although it was a cloudless, hot evening)! On went the galloping boots designed to protect front pony legs, from back pony feet. On went the high-powered bit designed as a supplemental braking system since it is not like I have ever bothered to install brakes on the Pony (OK, I took out the Happy Mouth and put in a full cheek. Look, this is my fantasy, and I think you should just go with me on it.)! On went the running martingale, a secondary supplemental braking system since I am fully aware that the Pony really does not have brakes (although I am not sure the trainer/therapist is aware of this niggling little detail). On went the special safety helmet designed to withstand the impact of a horse's hoof should you fall off and have your stridently galloping equine stomp on your head. On went the special safety vest designed to protect your ribs from snapping if afore mentioned stridently galloping equine tumbles head over heels and lands on you. Ah, the glory of cross-country! Cue the stirring music!

BOOM! Ah, my cell phone. The "1812 Overture" is suitably stirring, I believe. I picked up the phone. It was my husband, reminding me to pick up a gallon of milk on the way home.

But we were ready. My cross-country schooling buddy and I were all dressed up and looking for a place to go. Although if you know anything about eventing, you might be wondering, "What, are you planning to school for a ****[12] here?"

No, of course not. In our case all of this equipment, gear and apparatus were designed to protect us over fences the size of mole-hills. *Small* molehills.

While Beginner Novice is the lowest recognized eventing level in the United States, there are many venues that cater to the, well, the eventing challenged, as it were. That is, those of us for whom the fence height of 2'7" at Beginner Novice was just too darn high. My local horse park is one of those kind venues. So we were gearing up to jump what amounted to a couple of two-foot logs. No kidding. My horse park has a cute name for their lowest level: AVAGO—say it quickly with a cockney-like accent—like "Have a Go!" My train-er/therapist calls it the Micro Moron division, but I think that's just a loving reference to me.

And AVAGO was what I was aiming for—the two-foot division. I had been dreaming much bigger when I purchased the Pony way back in the early winter. I had dreams of qualifying for the Novice Championships, probably doing pretty well, if I do dream so myself, and then offering the Pony for sale for a modest amount consider-ing her great success and clear talent, but a major multiple of what I had paid for her. However, reality had intervened and I was pretty happy at this point to be shooting for the two-foot division.

The next event was in a couple of weeks, and I had already pre-registered thinking that this cross-country schooling plus my hunter show and two dressage shows somehow qualified me to compete at an actual real event. Of course, I would pose the question to the trainer/therapist after our cross-country school, but I was pretty confident. I mean, the Pony could jump over two-foot fences all day

---

12 A **** (pronounced "four star") is the penultimate level of eventing. I intro-duce the term (or the figure? What *would* you call "****"?) for two reasons. One, and the obvious one if you happen to know what a **** is, is that we were gearing up mightily for a pretty low-level cross-country school, so it's pretty funny. The second is the sheer entertainment value provided by this wacky naming convention. On the eso-teric nomenclature scale, "****" trumps "eventing" by a significant margin.

without ever stopping (a "stop" being a punishable offense in the eventing world). So carrying the weight of my two blue dressage ribbons, plus all of my cross-country gear, I was pretty cocky as we started to warm up for our cross-country school.

As we briefly touched on a few chapters ago, warm up for cross-country is usually done over three stadium-type fences that have been left in a field next to a cross-country course for just this purpose. This is how you warm up in an actual competition, so it makes sense to warm up this way for a cross-country school. The horses were pretty warmed up already from their dressage tests, so the trainer/therapist quickly initiated jumping.

Shockingly enough, it didn't go all that well. Jumping the Pony was not going all that well. She never stopped, which is a problem I may have alluded to in prior paragraphs. The Pony didn't stop at fences. She had never stopped at any fence I pointed her at. She was a wonder on four hooves about that. The heretofore skirted around problem was that she wouldn't stop *after* the fence either. She would mostly bolt off as fast as she could run. If I were in an indoor arena, the walls usually stopped her (which is not to say that she would run *through* a wall, but she could execute a pretty quick turn and be off running in another direction if I weren't right on top of her).

My experiences jumping her outside had been a little more unnerving. In a ring with a fence around it, I could usually use the fence to stop her. My few attempts at jumping cross-country fences by myself (this would be one of those, "kids, *don't* try this at home tricks"—cross-country schooling by yourself is very much frowned on for a million safety reasons) had resulted in some serious ground covered. She would happily trot up to the little two-foot log, *power* over it with all the thrust a pony her size could muster (which was actually a fair bit, particularly considering that she was hoisting a fair-sized adult over the log, too) and land at a full-out, hell-bent-for-leather gallop, half the time throwing in a significant buck for good measure.

I hadn't been exactly sharing all of this information with the trainer/therapist before today, thinking that maybe the problem was partially in my head and that with the trainer/therapist present, she could throw a rope around us and drag us back to the cross-country Golden Pathway.

The trainer/therapist pointed to a small crossrail warm-up fence and indicated that I should casually hop over it. I pointed the Pony toward it, offered a quick Hail Mary as a throwback to my younger days and prepared for the worst, which is about what happened. The Pony took one look at the crossrail, grinned an evil pony grin, gunned the engine and let loose full bore. She bolted toward the fence, leapt over all 18 inches of it with about four feet to spare, threw in a horrific buck and then flattened out in an all-out run for the horizon. I hung on by the skin of my teeth and dint of having a handful of mane as well as her breastplate clutched in my right hand. I finally managed to stop her by steering her into a very large tree.

I turned her back to the trainer/therapist with a sheepish grin on my face.

The trainer/therapist was just shaking her head ruefully. "Well," she said, "so that's what you meant when you kept saying, 'The Pony doesn't stop.'"

We tried again, with a repetition of the first leap. The trainer/therapist leapt into the fray, providing all kinds of advice and direction, which I valiantly tried to heed to no avail. The Pony was a runaway train—a small train with a not very powerful engine, but a runaway train nonetheless.

And the bucking after the fence was getting worse. That was one of those vicious cycle things that I was exacerbating. I knew the Pony was going to throw in a huge buck upon landing, so I braced myself ahead of time, which meant I was hanging onto her face as she was jumping, which pissed her off, which made her buck on landing. Do that a few times and see where it gets you.

The trainer/therapist was, of course, giving me proper direction to address the problem, but I kept thinking that I really wanted to see my children again and kept falling back into tragically bad habits that, while perhaps keeping me in the saddle, were not in any way going to solve the problems.

A couple more wildly out of control leaps and the trainer/therapist gave up. She threw her hands in the air and declared the current situation hopeless. It was back to the drawing board for us. There would no cross-country schooling for the Pony and me that day.

Sort of. If you will recall, I was not alone. I was riding with a friend who had actually taken the trainer/therapist's advice and bought herself a nice horse and was working with the trainer/therapist to get ready for the upcoming event. And as I was not alone in this, the cross-country school went on.

And to my horror, I discovered that day that there *is* an eventing division lower than Micro Moron. It is called "Lead Line." That would be where your trainer/therapist takes the reins and *leads* you around the cross-country course—for your own safety, of course.

CHAPTER 14

The $700 Pony Faces the Brutal Facts

With that cross-country school, our hopes of getting to an actual event seemed fairly dim. I decided I needed to take a short break from jumping. I called and scratched from the event I had entered. Since the Pony had been such a star at Dressage Debut Part Two, I decided I would enter one more dressage show. Interestingly enough, while it was a much better effort than our first show (although it was not hard to do better than that), it was nowhere near as good as our second, which was a little discouraging.

We did end up with a score that was sufficient to land us a spot as the Reserve Adult Walk/Trot Champion for the show series. Reserve Champion is like being the first runner up in the Miss America pageant. The Miss America people like to say "first runner up" so the second-place person doesn't feel, well, like they came in second. And "reserve champion" means basically the same thing: hey, you weren't champion but if the champion were to drop dead before we actually awarded the ribbons, we've got you in reserve!

And of course, "adult walk/trot." It just doesn't have the same ring to it as Prix St. Georges or Grand Prix now, does it?

The ribbon for this year end award was enormous—bigger than the Pony herself, maybe and all bright red and yellow—the traditional colors for reserve champion. While I secretly think blue is much nicer than red, it was a lovely ribbon and looked splendid on the wall where the Pony's slowly growing ribbon collection hung.

But the ribbon didn't bolster my spirits for long. I had a dream! A cross-country dream! And it was shattered. No pile of pretty dressage ribbons was going to make up for the fact that my eventing pony and I were not going to an event. I called the trainer/therapist feeling a little blue around the edges. Trying to sound more buoyant than I felt, I started with the good news: "So, she was reserve champion of the show series!"

The trainer/therapist was duly unimpressed.

"Walk/trot, right?"

"Um, yes."

"Did they include the juniors?"

The woman was sharp. "Um, no." Sighing, I confessed, "No, if they had included the juniors, she never would have gotten a year-end award."

"Ah, so you were second out of, what, three other walk/trot adults?"

"Five," I admitted. Really so unimpressive in the grand scheme of things. I sighed a deep sigh. "It's just not going that well, is it?"

"Well," the trainer/therapist said, "that depends on what you really want, doesn't it? If you really wanted to be out competing this year, you should have bought yourself a nice, made horse." She rather kindly didn't add, "like I told you to!"

"Green horses take time. I know you had this wild idea that you could show this pony in the spring and sell her, but I have to say, she was really, really green. A professional could probably have gotten her out in the spring. Or even you, maybe, before you had kids. And, well." She paused to think about what she wanted to say next. "If you want the truth, you're not riding all that well."

This was not really a surprise. Taking three years off from any sport is not a good idea. In the three years I had taken off, muscle tone and balance had all been lost. I knew things weren't that great, but surely they were getting better? Surely the Pony and I had made some progress lo these many months?

"Well, it's getting better, isn't it?" I asked.

"No. Your riding is really weak."

Ouch. That hurt. It wasn't a total surprise, of course, because the trainer/therapist *teaches* me on a semi-regular basis, and she had been *saying* these things all along. But I had the feeling I was really *hearing* them for the first time over the phone. It was almost like the cross-country schooling that wasn't had cleared up my hearing.

"Yeah," she said, "Next time you come over, we'll ride in the indoor and you can see for yourself in the mirrors."

And so I rode in the indoor. And so I did see for myself. We had been riding outdoors since the end of winter and I suppose I had been deluding myself. I rode pretty much every day, but when I saw—*really* saw—what was going on in the mirrors it was a revelation.

Frankly, it was pretty awful. My position was just, well, wrong. Mostly it was defensive. Since I was pretty unstable up there, I had apparently developed all of these physical tics that were designed to make me feel more secure. They didn't actually make me more secure, of course, and they made effective riding impossible. For example, I had developed this braced leg, so my legs were pretty much stuck out in front of me, which works really well if you are a Western pleasure rider or maybe even a saddleseat rider, but it is highly problematic for dressage. I mean, how can you put your leg on for a half halt if your leg is up near the horse's shoulder?

In addition, I was somehow pitching my upper body forward. When combined with the funky leg, I looked a little like a half-folded jackknife. This is a very common defensive riding posture, by the way. While very few people have ever been pitched off a horse backward (there are some who say it cannot be done, but I assure you, it can), it is an incredibly frightening thing to imagine, so most people, when they are a little on the timid side, are inclined to lean forward.

And then there was something weird going on with my hands. One of the key objectives I was working on with the Pony was to change her giraffe-like profile. The correct way to do this would be to use lots of leg and get her working from behind and allow her to come into contact with the bit, which should naturally elongate her profile, allow her to relax and eventually stretch down and into the bit.

But getting her to accept the contact has everything to do with my leg, which, if you will recall, was spending most of its time swinging loose, whacking her in the shoulder. Very ineffective. Apparently to compensate for my utter and absolute inability to use my leg, I was doing this weird wave-your-hands-high-in-the-air thing in a vain attempt to give the Pony some context for the stretching-down-into-the-bit thing I was looking for.

I finally stopped and stood staring at my still image in the mirror. Legs akimbo, sitting crooked with a weird, ineffective hand position. It was time to face the brutal facts.

Are you familiar with the Stockdale Paradox? It's a very interesting story. Jim Stockdale was a prisoner of war for almost eight years during Vietnam. Now there was a tough man. As he tells it there were two kinds of POWs: first, those who were optimistic and would sit around talking about how, for sure, they would be out for Christmas! And Christmas would pass. Then they would be sure they would be out for Easter! And Easter would pass. Eventually all of these people died. As Stockdale would tell it, optimism kills.[13]

---

[13] Stockdale's exact quote was that they would die of a "broken heart." Credit for elucidating the Stockdale Paradox should go to Jim Collins of *Good to Great* fame.

The second kind of POW was more of a realist. They were the ones who confronted the brutal facts of the situation they were in. They dealt in day-to-day survival instead of wishful thinking. They also retained faith that they would prevail in the end, but they faced the brutal facts, and they did eventually make it home.

I would generally be the antithesis of a Stockdale Paradox kind of thinker. I mean, I am fairly bright and sunny and energetic. And blond. Did I mention blond? I am not sure there are too many blond adherents to the Stockdale Paradox, but it was time to face the brutal facts. Bright, shiny blond optimism was not doing me a blessed bit of good right now.

"Oh. My. Gosh. I can't believe what I mess I am!" I was still staring in the mirror. "What are we going to do?!" The Golden Pathway was totally eluding me. I was spending way too much time out in the middle of nowhere, and I needed more guidance and direction.

The trainer/therapist nodded not unsympathetically, "I've been trying to tell you." She hesitated, "I do have suggestion. I'm not sure if you are up for it, but I do think that if we work together on this, we can at least get you to a place where you might be able to do one of those AVAGO events before the end of the season. There are one or two scheduled for November, I think."

November? It was August! "So what are you thinking?" I asked a little hesitantly. Facing the brutal facts was one thing, but the trainer/therapist could be tough.

"Well," she said, "I think it is time for you and the Pony to go to boot camp," with which she leaned over and took away my stirrups.

CHAPTER 15

The $700 Pony Goes to Boot Camp

Now, I don't know about you, but I look forward to riding without stirrups with about the same level of enthusiasm as I would an invasive dental procedure without anesthetic. It is painful and not only results in extreme discomfort during riding, but also often for days afterward. But to really learn how to ride well, you need to have an independent seat. Probably the quickest way to develop a great independent seat is a lot of time in the saddle without stirrups working on improved security and balance.

But it is no fun, and it's really hard. Frankly, my seat was so *dependent* that I hadn't been riding without stirrups because I really thought I would just fall off. I had been "planning" to do some work without stirrups, but I just hadn't gotten around to it. Or something like that.

The trainer/therapist's idea, which was a good one in principle, was that I should spend the next month roaming about the 130 hilly acres of my farm without stirrups. Now, I don't like to ride for more than a few seconds at a time without stirrups, so the idea of spending a month, not only a long period of time, but up hill and over dale and, in general, riding all over the place was not my cup of tea.

"Hey," I shouted. "Give those back!"

"Nope," she said. "It's for your own good. I'm tired of listening to you whine, and the only thing that is going to make all of this better," she gestured to me, the Pony and my trailer, "is if you get your act together first. So no stirrups for a month. Then call me."

And she walked off, holding my stirrups in her hand. Of course, she was right. I faced the brutal facts and headed home sans stirrups.

And so began Pony Boot Camp. The deal was even better than just no stirrups for a month, though, because as it turned out one of the trainer/therapist's regular boarders was leaving with her horse for the month of September. The trainer/therapist's thought was that I should bring the Pony to her barn for the month. I was going to be away for a week during that time, so the trainer/therapist would ride the Pony for that week to try to undo the damage I had inflicted on her. Upon my return, I would be able to use the indoor with mirrors and have twice weekly lessons until the end of the month. The plan was then to enter the last AVAGO of the season. My swan song, as it were, for the season that wasn't.

The $700 Pony and I began our new training regime bright and early the next morning at my farm where she had formally taken up residence. After spending two years on The Amish Men's waiting list, they had finally arrived and rebuilt our barn! And while it was missing a few of the amenities traditionally associated with the modern horse barn, like running water, electricity and lights, it was now the place the Pony called home. The stalls were incredible. The falling down barn had been returned to all of its former glory, and the Amish Men had done a magnificent job of carving some beautiful horse space out of the old dairy cow area. The barn still needed to be painted and we hadn't gotten around to installing any real fencing yet, but we were managing to contain the Pony within our 130 acres and, painters were scheduled for some eventual date.

The sun was shining in the newly carved out windows, casting a glow on the fresh wood of the Amish-built stalls. The Pony swished her gorgeous tail in the glinting sunbeams, and I plopped the saddle with no stirrups on her back and put on her bridle.

And thusly I was presented with the first puzzle of the morning. How in the heck was I going to heave myself up on her back? Now she is a Pony, which makes her not all that tall. But I am not all that tall, either, or I would not be able to ride a Pony. The usual mounting procedure for English riders is to stand the horse next to a mounting block. The ostensive objective of the mounting block is to take weight off of the stirrup so the saddle does not slip and become crooked on the horse's back. The real reason we all use a mounting block is that we are too old and fat to heave ourselves up without it.

Sensible people use a solidly built, wooden mounting block, the objective of which is to keep you and or horse from falling on your faces. My mounting block is an old broken cinder block left over from barn construction. It is pretty low to the ground because I generally don't need all that much height to get up on the Pony.

I hopped up on my old cinder block and realized there was no way in heck I was getting up on that Pony from that height. My leg just doesn't have that much swing. If I were a Rockette at Radio City Music Hall, maybe. But, if I were a Rockette, I would have been too tall to ride a Pony, wouldn't I? Life is full of these trade-offs.

Sighing, I looked all over for something high enough that I could stand on that the Pony could stand next to that would enable me to get on her without her losing her somewhat fragile mind.

Nothing.

We left the barn area and headed back to the house. Aha! The car! I could stand on my car bumper! The bumper was the right height, but I was having a heck of a time getting the Pony to stand anywhere near the bumper. I could get her only within a foot or two, which was not quite close enough. And the bumper was not quite wide enough for me to stand on. So I could slither up, but when I tried to drag her over, I would slither off. This went on for what felt like at least four hours, when I heard a knocking sound. I looked up and there was my husband in the window, laughing. Pretty hard by the looks of it.

I shot him a dirty look and slithered up again. Humiliation lent some wings to my otherwise earthbound butt and with a rather large grunt, I was able to fling myself onto the Pony's back. It was not pretty, and the Pony was not pleased about it.

I was really, really not happy without those stirrups. I was adrift up there, which I think was part of the point of the exercise. I mean,

I should have felt snug as a bug in a rug, and I was feeling more like a fried egg on a Teflon pan. Slip, slide, slip slide.

Ah, well, I sighed to myself, facing the brutal facts. This must be done and it has got to get better.

So the Pony and I set off to explore the boundaries of our farm and work on developing an independent seat. It was a lovely late summer morning. The sun was peeping over the horizon, the dew was glistening on our maturing hay fields, getting ready for the second cut. And I was feeling about as secure as a window washer on the 35th floor who left his safety belt at home: not very safe at all.

It may be worth mentioning that while we have a wealth of geographic variety on our farm, flat land would be one thing in rather short supply.

Clutching a little bit of mane, I pointed the Pony up one of our hills and set off at a trot. Sighing mightily, I could feel my thighs start to burn instantly. But again, this was the point of the exercise. The Pony, a little fresh in the cooler morning air was happy enough to trot off and then happy enough to raise her head straight up in the air when she saw a deer in the corner. She stepped sideways in a tiny bit of a fright spook, and I fell off.

I slipped off like it was what I was intending to do, truth be told, just like a 2-year old human slipping down the slide at the playground. Just, poof! On the ground. The Pony, gentle soul that she inherently is, stopped, a little startled by the fact that I had disembarked so unusually in the middle of our journey. I held on to the reins, but realized that having the Pony in hand was only part of the victory. What was missing was a way to get back on.

Luckily there was an old stone wall not too far away. I dragged the still blinking Pony (*What just happened?*) over to the wall and with much grunting, but at least without an audience, I heaved myself back up onto that Teflon saddle.

Muscles throbbing already from the sheer ignominy of riding without stirrups and then the jolt of the fall, we hobbled up the hill, me clinging like a drunken monkey to a tree branch in a Category 5 hurricane.

We only saw one more deer, and I only fell off one more time. So endeth day one.

Repeat ad infinitum. After a week of this horror I called the trainer/therapist.

"So, how's boot camp going?" she asked.

"I haven't hit the dirt this often …" I paused to reflect. "… ever." And it was true. I have never much been one for falling off. I mean, it's not something you generally set out to do in the course of a daily ride, and I have always been one of those "ounce of prevention" riders.

"You're falling off?" she asked, a little surprised.

"How about four times today?" I sighed. Ignoble doesn't begin to describe how I was feeling. Every bone in my body ached; every muscle felt like it was pulsing to some hidden Latin salsa beat. Ouch. Ouch. Ouch. My riding muscles, which I had apparently not been using at all over the past eight months, were all on high alert. Hey, down here! Ouch! Pinch! The different parts of my body that kept hitting the ground as I slithered off again and again were yelling in protest. My knees, my poor old knees! I would occasionally land on my feet, so my poor knees were probably suffering the worst. At least when I landed on my shoulder, it was too numb to protest any more.

One of the more interesting phenomena coming to light during this period of torture was the awakening of the Pony's sense of humor. She has always been a shy and skittish soul, perhaps too timid to laugh openly in public. Not that horses actually laugh, mind you, but some horses have a very obvious sense of humor. The Pony did not.

But all of this flailing about had apparently opened a door for the Pony. She had reached a stage where I believe she was enjoying my pain. We would be trotting along, with me groaning in pain, and she would sneak a glance back at me, bat her long, long eyelashes a few times, and then ever so coyly, and sometimes I swear even in slow motion just to enhance her own enjoyment of the moment, slip herself sideways and snort the equivalent of an equine giggle as I slipped off.

Merde! I would yell, shaking my fists at the gods of riding. "This is supposed to be FUN!" And then the struggle to find some way to slither back up onto that Teflon saddle on the back of that Mt. Denali size pony.

But it was getting better. Even I had to admit that while the whole process was hideously torturous, there was a marked and rapid improvement in my riding. I was actually using my legs, my balance was getting better and while I would not go so far as to say that my seat was "independent," it was at least beginning to show signs that one day it would be able to live on its own. I was riding better than I had since prior to the addition of the two wee ones to my life.

Oh, there was the occasional speed bump, of course. The day I decided to add bell boots to the mix comes immediately to mind. Bell boots, for the uninitiated, are plastic covers that you put over a horse's front feet in order to protect their front heels from their hind feet.

The Pony had taken to knocking her front feet with her back feet (technically called "forging"), and I decided to put bell boots on her to protect her from (a) knocking herself and creating a huge "ouch" and (b) accidentally stepping on a front shoe and pulling it off—a big no-no particularly when your farrier is hours away and doesn't make house calls for insignificant pony clients who have popped off a shoe.

With my usual forethought, I thought, "Hmm, the Pony is not very good at new things. I really should let her wear them out for the night before I ride her with them on."

And as usual, that just did not happen. I called my local tack shop that had exactly the thing I needed, put them on hold, had my poor long-suffering husband pick them up ("*$30* for a pair of boots for the Pony?? Do they have Vibram soles?" he asked. Oh, I thought, good thing I don't have you stop and pick up blankets!). By the time he got home with them, it was dark and too late to put them on the Pony.

The first time she wore them was when I slithered up on her, Pony Boot Camp, Day 13. The good news was that by day 13, I was really riding a lot better. The bad news was she was totally convinced that the bell boots were from the Devil himself and were destined somehow to crawl up her legs, slit open her belly and eat her for lunch.

When I first put them on in the wash stall, she peered suspiciously down at her feet and shifted her weight a little. When I walked her out with them on, she staggered around as though she was going to drop to the ground. You know, for a $700 pony, the thing has an unerring sense of drama.

Once I was up on her back, she did OK as long as we were walking. She was picking up each foot and putting it down with a little shake, almost as though she were trying to shake the bell boot off and give it a good stomp for good measure. But once we started trotting, the Pony Predator Alarm went off big time. Alert! Alert! Predator attached to *left foot*! Alert! Alert! Predator attached to *right foot*!

The Pony's radar ears swiveled, left, right, left, right to the ever increasing tempo of her trot. I knew I was in trouble right away and tried to stop her, but my balance, while better than it had been 13 days prior, was still not good enough to really sit up and let her know it was time to stop. I tried voice commands, but the Almighty Voice of Survival was ringing louder in her furry ears than my pitiful little, "STOP, PONY, STOP!!"

Increasing her speed and length of stride with each step, the Pony was quickly turning into an unstoppable dynamo, and I was in no position to do anything about it.

The faster she went, the harder she struck the ground with each step. It seemed that she was attempting to dislodge these potentially predatory things attached to her feet. As she whipped up into a canter and then shifted into fifth, I silently cursed the Happy Mouth bit she was wearing. A gag would have done wonders for me right about then. Or a fence I could aim her at. Or even a really big tree. But we were out in the middle of a huge field. She was an object in motion, and she was planning to stay in motion.

I was clinging fairly well up until this point and since we were heading uphill, I did figure she would run out of steam fairly quickly. So I hung on, optimistically thinking that as long as she got tired before we started back down the hill, all would end well.

Nope. No chance of that.

What happened next was yet another out scene out of "Wild Kingdom run amuck." We ran into a fox. It was truly one of my stranger wild animal encounters, and I have to say that I have had a few strange wild animal encounters.

It went something like this: we were motoring up this hill, seriously out of control, when the Pony stepped down and her bell-boot-encased foot landed on the tail of a fox. Yes, indeedy, that was one unhappy fox.

I would like to point out that this story demonstrates a clear difference between predators and prey in the wild. There would have been no chance that we would have had the same experience with the average, say, deer, bunny rabbit or wild turkey. These critters have built-in radar that is working all the time. A bunny rabbit on this self-same hill would have felt the thundering echoes of the Pony galloping out of control long ago and found a safer place to be. I mean, if you are prey, your whole life is about winning a little game I call "Pass the DNA." You win if you reproduce, and you lose if you get stomped to death by a rampaging pony.

But the predators? Well, they are a little less wily. A fox does a lot of sneaking, but there's not a whole heck of a lot sneaking up on *him*, so he's a little less inclined to be paying attention. This particular individual was definitely not on high alert. The Homer Simpson of the fox world, when the Pony slammed her hoof down on the end of his tail, you could just about hear the "D'OH!" as he popped up his head and considered, way, way, too late that perhaps this was not the best resting place for his little fox self at this particular moment in time.

The Pony, shocked out of her mind at the idea of a fox under her foot, executed a Serengeti Slide the breadth and depth of which I had never experienced before. I fell off. I did not land on the fox, although I sure wished I had. The ground was hard. The fox would have broken my fall somewhat, and although I might have squished his little fox life out of existence, it would have served him right for not noticing the Pony pounding toward him up the hill.

The fox, meanwhile, let out a shriek that was bone chilling, not that you can much blame him. I have had the Pony tromp on my foot when I have boots on, so I can only imagine how his poor naked tail felt. I could see from my vantage points, which started out up high on top of the Pony and ended up down low near to where the fox was, that it was just, in fact, his tail that the Pony had tromped. He gathered his wits quickly, gave me a very dirty look for disturbing his morning snooze and fled off into the underbrush.

Thankfully, that was actually my last parting of ways with the Pony during the stirrupless time of boot camp. All of that miserable riding without stirrups was really paying off and I have to say that by the end of the month, I was riding almost as well (which is still to say, not all that great, but certainly better than pre-boot camp) as I had before I took three years off.

Phase two of Pony boot camp was to deposit the Pony at trainer/therapist's for a month. The trainer/therapist would ride her for the first week while I spent the week in Portugal with my husband. (Hey, I needed time to recover from all that time without stirrups, didn't I?) Husband had a business meeting, and I decided that I needed to tag along to, um, help. Or hang out and drink port for a week. Whatever.

I was a little sneaky about the whole thing, though. When I dropped the Pony off, I told her she was going to spend a month at the "Pony Spa" and I left for a week of touring vineyards. Perhaps it was a little mean spirited of me, but I considered it revenge for the last half dozen or so times I hit the ground.

I left the Pony with clear instructions that she was to behave and demonstrate her best pony manners for all of my friends at the barn, most of whom had not seen me but for the occasional birth announcement in several years. I probably should have purchased a copy of "How to Win Friends and Influence Enemies" prior to departure, since it became evident upon my return that the Pony had not read the book on her own. Her behavior was so short of exemplary that on my return, she was threatened with expulsion.

She apparently exhibited quite nasty mareish behavior while in her stall. She kicked at her neighbors at dinnertime and generally harassed them when it was not. Her behavior was so not nice that when the weather was nice enough, she got kicked out all day … and all night.

The poor trainer/therapist was not all that enthusiastic about riding her. I mean, she has some really nice horses to ride. But she is a consummate professional and did, in fact, ride the Pony every day while I was gone. Upon my return and after convincing the trainer/therapist to let the ill-mannered Pony stay the remainder of her scheduled time in boot camp, she gave me the tour of the new-and-improved $700 Pony. Although for what I paid for that week that she rode the Pony, I was seriously thinking of changing her name.

The trainer/therapist hopped on the Pony first to demonstrate. "Look," she said, with absolutely no sarcasm, which made me feel a little embarrassed, "She has brakes!" And indeed she did! After months of my own unsuccessful attempts at installation, the trainer/therapist had accomplished brakes on the Pony in just a few short days!

And there was more! As part of the braking package, the trainer/therapist declared, "She even has a fully functional half halt!" Wow! It really was impressive. The trainer/therapist demonstrated a few steps of leg yield, a little shoulder-in and even had a few nice canter transitions. And the best, best, best was that the trainer/therapist had been jumping the Pony—quietly and without too much fuss.

She had made a ton of progress in a week. And now it was up to me.

My time in the saddle sans stirrups had made a dramatic improvement in my position and consequently my effectiveness. Between the twice weekly visits to the Golden Pathway under the Trainer/Therapists' direction and my riding time in between where I made great use of the mirrors, I was able make up for much lost time. And as I worked assiduously over the next three weeks to make the remainder of boot camp pay off, the Pony and I made tremendous progress.

While at the trainer/therapist's we were able to conquer jumping a tiny two-foot stadium course, plonking over microscopic cross-country fences and refining our already championship quality walk/trot dressage. All in all it was an eminently satisfying three weeks, made all the more satisfying when the trainer/therapist pronounced us ready to enter AVAGO.

CHAPTER 16

The Final Chapter About the $700 Pony

And so we entered our first and last event of the season. November is typically a pretty cold and sadly tragic month here in the fine state of New Jersey, so I was not looking forward to it. I mean, I was, of course, because I entered. But I wasn't because the odds of the day dawning cold and gray with rain, sleet or snow in the forecast was an all-too-real possibility. But it was the last, last chance I was going to have to actually event the Pony this year.

The riding signs were all in alignment. The trainer/therapist was nodding more and more and shaking her head in disgust less. The Golden Dust sprinkled at the end of our lessons seemed to hang around longer and longer. The Pony officially had brakes with me and her half halts, if not exactly Olympic caliber, were happily functional. And while her canter work would not be winning her any awards this year, the beauty of the division we had entered was that it was, well, a walk/trot division.

Those of you who are more familiar with the sport of eventing are cackling right now. "*What?*" you snort, wiping tears of laughter from your eyes. *Eventing* with no *galloping*? Are you crazy? That would be like eating Häagen-Dazs Frozen Yogurt! I mean why bother? The whole point of eventing is that it is like a James Dean movie! Fast, furious and a little dangerous!

True, all true. But the only division the trainer/therapist would let me enter was AVAGO! And while we would be able to do some semblance of a gallop cross-country, the dressage test was our old friend Intro Test B, which, as the Adult Reserve Champion of the Intro Division, I am proud to say I had memorized and the Pony could execute with some degree of obedience and suppleness.

And about that galloping during the AVAGO cross-country phase, well, we would need to be careful. The fences that the Pony and I would be so boldly launching ourselves over were so small that my husband with a 35-pound child on his back could leap over every one of them himself. So there was a real fear that if we got rolling too fast we might trip.

The timing of the event was a little off in that it was not scheduled until a week after we left pony boot camp. Which means that the Pony was back living with me for that week. And I have to say that the stars were not in alignment for *that* event. One issue was that, while there was more electricity in the barn than when she left, it had still not migrated to the point where I actually had lights or electric in the part of the barn where the Pony lived. While not such an issue during the long summer days, I was not looking forward to the dark mornings of October with no lights in my barn.

And then, well, have you ever had one of *those* weeks? I did the week the Pony was coming home. You know the kind of week I am talking about.

Something like your husband calls you and tells you that he's bringing home some baby pigs to grow into big pigs that will eventually end up in your freezer and you say, "Over my dead body will you put pigs in the stalls the Amish Men built for horses!" and then there are pigs in your barn, in fact in the stalls that the Amish Men built for horses and the pigs immediately root up the rubber mats and dig holes in the stone dust underneath thereby mitigating the work the Amish Men did to level the stalls and put down the mats for horses and somehow, you still seem to be living and breathing? Yeah, it was one of those weeks.

So my glorious barn, the gorgeously-restored-by-Amish-Hands barn is a pigsty. For real. Which, by the way, is very different from when I say my *house* is a pigsty. And to clarify, my house *is* a pigsty. People ask me all the time, "Girl, how do you do it!? How do you manage the farm and the chickens and riding and the newspaper column and writing a book and the children and all the other stuff you do? *How do you do it?"*

Easy. I never clean my house, cook for my husband or do laundry. I'm real friendly, but you might want to stay downwind on a breezy day. So although on the surface it might appear that I might have some affinity for these porcine additions to our farm in that I am content to claim that I live in a pigsty, I was being figurative. The pigs were literal.

But it has long been established in our household that if my husband really has a hankering for something, he is going to get it. Basically he is a great salesman. Despite the fact that I know the word "no" in 13 languages, he has the kind of tenacity rarely seen in *homo sapiens*. Rat terriers, maybe. But he just hangs on until I either say yes or he *thinks* I have said yes.

When the opportunity came up for us to get a few free little pigs to raise, I wanted to say no. I tried to say no. I thought maybe I even *had* said no. But the pigs arrived and took up residence in the barn. And neither the $700 Pony nor I were happy. Can you blame her? Or me? The chickens, she was used to and even liked, I think. There was even one that would perch on her back on warm days, a chestnut pony and a chestnut laying hen enjoying a soak in the sun together.

But the pigs? Well, first, they were babies, so they made a lot of noise. And second, it didn't take long before the barn stopped smelling like a $700 Pony and started smelling like pigs. We just didn't like it.

But life goes on. The pigs arrived, the Pony returned home from pony boot camp with a week to go before the big eventing debut and my husband left—for California—for the week. Now, this is not unusual. The man travels. It's how he supports us, and I am pretty used to it.

But his comings and goings tend to complicate things a bit.

First off, when he is gone, I do not ride, as there is no one to watch the two children. And while the workload on our farm is, well, certainly not much in the grand scheme of things, it all must be accomplished with the two wee children in tow. As per the prior sentence, there's no one to watch the children.

So, the Pony was home and I needed to feed her twice a day, clean her stall and turn her out and bring her in based on weather. Plus feed and water the chickens, collect the eggs and feed and water the pigs. The good news and what made all of this actually doable was the fact that we were experiencing some extremely nice weather in early November. It was getting up into the high 70s during the day, and the wee children and I were able to head out early in the mornings without our coats.

In fact, my M.O. during this lovely weather streak was to hustle everyone out of bed for a quick breakfast and then strap them into the double stroller with their PJs still on and head down to the barn. The PJs are important because the children like to play with the chickens while I feed and muck. So we return to the house with two little poo-covered children. Then it is bath time. And because I was mucking about, too, it was easier for me to just head down in my PJs, too.

Now, in the horse world, there are lots of people who muck in their PJs. No kidding. It's just easier to get that stuff dirty doing your morning chores, then drop it in the wash and you in the shower and start the rest of the day with fresh clothes. So PJs are *de rigueur* for people who have houses and barns that are far enough off the road that they are safe from detection by their neighbors.

The first morning that I was alone, the two wee children and I ate our quick breakfast, and I strapped their little pajama-clad bottoms into the double stroller. I slipped my muck boots on over my pajamas and off we went. It just so happened that I was wearing my really Cute Cowgirl Roping PJs. My husband had gotten them for me for Christmas and I have to say I loved them! They were flannel and warm and had little pictures of cowgirls roping cows and riding bucking broncos all over them. While in my general life I prefer to keep my horsy things themed more "eventing" or "dressage," the PJs were so cute! The bonus was that they were my young son's favorites, too.

I'm a little embarrassed to say this, although, with all that has been shared thus far, this is a pretty minor morsel: we even have a song that we sing when I wear the pajamas. It's a little ditty called "Poor Lonesome Cowboy." The lyrics as written by the original poor lonesome cowboy were pretty simple:

> I ain't got no father,
> I ain't got no father,
> I ain't got no father
> To buy the clothes I wear.

> Chorus: I'm a poor, lonesome cowboy,
> I'm a poor lonesome cowboy,
> I'm a poor lonesome cowboy,
> And a long ways from home.

I have no idea what the actual tune is, but it's not like my three-year-old is going to be checking to see if I got it right, is he? No indeed! So I made up a cowboy twangy kind of tune that worked really well. And then we made up the words as we went along. For example, that morning as I was filling the pig feeder, I sang at high volume and with great gusto but with very little actual singing talent with my three-year-old piping along in that tuneless way three-year-olds pipe:

> I ain't got no husband
> I ain't got no husband
> I ain't got no husband
> To fill this pig trough for me!

Chorus: I am a poor lonesome mommy
I am a poor lonesome mommy
I am a poor lonesome mommy
All alone on the farm!

And so on. It was a hoot, and we were bellowing this little ditty at the top of our lungs while we collected the eggs, which is probably why I didn't hear the sound of car tires crunching on the gravel in my courtyard. We weren't going to be lonesome for much longer.

Barn painters. And as the barn is fairly large, it was a largish crew who pulled in while I was belting out my lonesomeness—wearing my Cute Cowgirl Roping Pajamas.

They were fairly professional about the whole thing and acted as though they came across women who hung out in their barns bellowing cowboy ditties wearing their Cute Cowgirl Roping Pajamas every day, which I am sure they did not. But that is neither here nor there. They came and stuck ladders up all over my barn, thereby making it very hard to maneuver around,

As much as the advent of the barn painters left me wishing I could change out of the Cute Cowgirl Roping Pajamas, it just didn't make sense to haul the children back to the house, change clothing and haul everyone back down again, so despite my utter and complete embarrassment, I just set about to finishing my barn chores while the painter men got to work.

Mucking the stall turned out to be the hardest bit, mostly because my husband had taken my one and only muck bucket, scrubbed it out and filled it with water for the pigs. Couple of issues here: the first is that the muck bucket was my sole means of moving dirty stall bedding from the $700 Pony's stall. It was now full of water inside the stall where the little, tiny pigs were secured.

The idea, I think, had been to provide them with an emergency water supply in case they drank all or tipped over their more little-tiny-piggy-appropriate water source. Unfortunately, if the little, tiny pigs in fact executed a stupid move like depriving themselves of

their little piggy water source, the only way they were going to be able to reach high enough to use the muck bucket would be if one stood on the other's back, which seemed fairly unlikely to me. Of course, if they did focus all of their pig brain cells on achieving this end and actually managed to execute the one-pig-on-top-of-the-other move, it seemed there was an excellent chance that the one on top would lose his balance, tip into the muck bucket and drown.

But I needed to muck her stall at some point over the next week, and my only way to move manure was locked up tight. But while it was a hurdle that must be overcome, it was not the biggest issue of the day.

No, actually the biggest issue of the day, once we got over the fact that my three-year-old-almost-housebroken son decided in the middle of all of this he needed to pee, and we had to maneuver ourselves around the barn painters, who, by the way, were smoking around my barn and using my driveway as though it were part of a 130-acre ashtray. Once *that* little issue had been resolved, and I made a note that I needed to order a ton or so of pig and chicken feed and got the 10 dozen eggs or so in the egg basket (bloody heavy and hard to push the double stroller up the hill carrying the eggs, too, but what is a mom to do?), I realized the $700 Pony had a fat ankle.

Merde!

Our first and only event was on Saturday! I wasn't going to be able to ride with my husband gone all week anyway, but now this! How in heck was I going to find time to cold hose her four or five times a day, which would have been my M.O. pre addition of the wee ones. And Bute! I had to get my hands on some Bute! And a rulebook—when would I have to stop giving her Bute? And what— I shuddered at this thought—what if it were something *serious*!

There was no doubt that I was a little close to the edge and not thinking too clearly. Taking care of a farm and two small children is stressful. To be discovered by barn painters in your Cute Cowgirl Roping Pajamas was added stress. To discover that the Pony might have injured herself and that we might be SOL for our final event opportunity of the season was really, really stressful. Luckily, I had my cell phone. I called The Instigator. Yeah, it was 8 am, but she has a farm and two small children. She picked up on the first ring and I just started talking.

"The Pony has a fat ankle! What am I going to do? I'm all alone with the children and the pigs and the chickens and the barn painters are here and I am standing here in *my Cute Cowgirl Roping Pajamas,* and how am I going to cold hose her with the children? And there's poo everywhere! Pig poo and chicken poo and Pony poo and the muck bucket is full of water and and … and …" I barely paused for breath, but the Instigator was quiet, "And … and … and …" and this is what I was really afraid of, "what … what … what if the ankle is something *serious*! What am I going to do?!"

At this point, The Instigator's husband asked if I perhaps wanted to speak with his wife.

Ooooh. That was embarrassing.

I had a moment to collect myself while she got on the phone. A little calmer, I reiterated the story minus a few of the hysterics. The Instigator is a bit like the trainer/therapist in that she is a straight shooting, pretty logical person. She made a list of quick practical suggestions for dealing with the immediate issues and then suggested that I put the Pony on a lunge line to get a better idea of what might be going on with the ankle then give her Bute and just leave her alone. "And no," she said, "It's not serious."

"But how do you know?" I wailed.

She was quite reassuring, "The $700 Pony is a pony. That makes her, by definition, indestructible. She probably did it on purpose just to freak you out." And with that she hung up.

The Instigator was right, of course. It was a little fat ankle. Nothing to get upset about. A deep breath would do me a world of good right now. It was such a pretty morning, I noted as I looked around at the barn painter men working on my barn.

I clipped a lunge line on the $700 Pony's halter and with her in one hand, the egg basket in another, all somehow while pushing the double stroller, I dragged the entire brood up to the flattest part of our farm—a small area in the orchard. Parking the stroller under an apple tree, I put the Pony on a 20-meter circle and lunged her for a few minutes to see where we stood with the ankle.

As the $700 Pony trotted quietly in a 20-meter circle, I took another deep breath and looked around. It really was a lovely moment. It was so unseasonably warm for October. It felt lovely standing there in my cozy, warm Cute Cowgirl Roping Pajamas. The sun was still low on the morning horizon, and it was glinting off of the Pony's gorgeous blond tail. The Pony was stretching down just a little and using her hind end even though she just had a halter on. She was relaxed and happy. She looked pretty sound, too, even on the puffy ankle. But what really struck me was that she looked *relaxed* and *happy*. My children were quietly playing under the tree, possibly getting ready to use the just-collected eggs as ammunition in a yolk war, but they were pretty relaxed and happy, too.

And suddenly, so was I.

Have you ever had one of those moments? Where one second you were worrying your life like a Rat Terrier gnawing on a tennis ball? And then there's some epiphany thing? And then it's like you are suddenly 50 pounds lighter? Almost light enough to float away? That's how I felt. And there were no controlled substances involved in this transformation—just the $700 Pony, looking so relaxed and happy.

As I got to thinking about it, standing there in my chicken-poo-spotted pajamas, it was just about a year since I had plunked down my $700. I shook my head laughing to myself about the dreams I'd had a year ago. I probably should have cried, thinking about where I actually was, versus where I wanted to be. But the sun was shining, my children were playing and the $700 Pony, well, she was relaxed and happy, so I just laughed.

I could go on and tell you all about our first event. About how I ran down to the barn 14 times a day and cold hosed her that week until her hoof about wrinkled up and fell off. And how much I worried about bone chips and torn ligaments and rotated coffin bones and how much Bute I could give her without killing her and all assorted ills for another 24 hours, which was about how long it took for the swelling to go down. Or about how the eventing weekend dawned gorgeous and unseasonably warm for November in New Jersey. And how the beautifully (professionally) clipped and (non-professionally) braided $700 Pony was able to luxuriate in the sun

I could tell you about the Haflinger stallion she met at the event and fell hopelessly in love with. And who had the most beautiful blond tail I had ever seen beside the $700 Pony's. It made me think that maybe the $700 Pony was maybe a Quarterflinger.

And about how she put in the loveliest dressage test, which gave us the lowest score of the day—which I probably should have mentioned earlier, means she was in first place after this phase.

And how she galloped quietly around the ultra-mini cross-country course, all relaxed and happy, and didn't stop, fall down, toss me off or do anything else that would have added penalty points. It was just fun.

And how she did the same in stadium, all relaxed and happy. And it was just fun. And, thusly, how she won her first and only event of the season. But, it's not really all that important in the grand scheme of things, is it? The winning, I mean. What's important is that we had fun. Both of us.

Although, I must say, the blue ribbon is beautiful.

Acknowledgements

Achieving life dreams rarely happen in a vacuum, and it is with incredible gratitude that I acknowledge the importance of the following people in the writing and publication of this book:

Thanks of course to my husband, Jeff, who really does make it all possible. And to Tom and Hope, the long suffering 48 Orphan Puppy Equivalents who will one day look with horror upon this tome.

Huge thanks are owed to my Mom who provided significant distraction for the 48 Orphan Puppy Equivalents during the time I was transcribing the trials and tribulations of the $700 Pony. And to my Dad, who supported my Mom while I wrote.

Many thanks are due to Liz Gallen, the long suffering trainer/therapist and the ladies of Blue Heron Farm who provided editing support and who, while they shake their heads in dismay every time I roar down the driveway in a cloud of dust, continue to put up with me with relative good humor.

Thanks, of course, to The Instigator, Paige DiRoberto, who never ceases to inspire and amaze me.

Thanks to Margaret Odgers, who paved the way for horse humor writers everywhere, and who introduced me to the indefatigable Beth Carnes of Half Halt Press, without whom there would be no book.

Thanks to Gary Maholic who with his usual incredible patient good nature put up with some serious cyber nagging and dug up a long lost chapter for me. And, a personal aside to Gary's Mom, *"Mrs. Maholic, saving stuff is good!"*

Special thanks are due to the *Chronicle of the Horse* bulletin board. I'm not exactly sure how I can ever fully express my gratitude to the vast mass of horse folk who make up what is affectionately known as the CoTH BB. This group of twenty thousand strong horse people provided a venue for my writing and then encouraged, cajoled, threatened and ultimately provided the impetus for me to take my words from cyberspace to the printed page. To all of you, I cannot thank you enough. Oh, and DillansMom, congratulations on the successful achievement of your 2004 goal: you convinced RR to write a book!

And the Pony? Are you wondering if she has been sold down the river yet to finance my big eventing dreams? No, no, she most certainly has not. The PT Cruiser dream is no more—replaced by a little pony with a big heart. If you happen to be eventing on the east coast in the next few years and see a little chestnut pony with a gorgeous blond tail streak by, give us a wave and a cheer, will you?

Ellen Broadhurst
Reynard Ridge

About the Author

Ellen Broadhurst is a refugee from the professional world of marketing. She now lives and writes on her 130 acre farm in New Jersey, along with her husband, two wee children, one psycho mutt, an untold number of free range chickens and, of course, the $700 Pony.